BOBBY FLAY'S
BOY MEETS
GRILL

BOBBY FLAY'S

BOY MEETS GRILL

WITH MORE THAN 125 BOLD NEW RECIPES

Bobby Flay
and
Joan Schwartz

Photographs by
Tom Eckerle

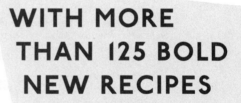

HYPERION

NEW YORK

Grateful acknowledgment is made to:

Clarkson N. Potter/Publishers for permission to reprint the recipe Shrimp Stock, which appeared in Bobby Flay's *From My Kitchen to Your Table* by Bobby Flay and Joan Schwartz (copyright © 1998 Boy Meets Grill, Inc.); Jack McDavid, for permission to use the recipe Jack's Turkey Porterhouse Steaks, adapted from Jack McDavid; Allen Susser, for permission to use the recipe title Mango Ketchup.

Copyright © 1999 Bobby Flay

Photographs © 1999 by Tom Eckerle

Library of Congress Cataloging-in-Publication Data

Flay, Bobby.
   [Boy meets grill]
   Bobby Flay's boy meets grill : with more than 125 bold new recipes / Bobby Flay and Joan Schwartz. — 1st ed.
      p.   cm.
   Includes index.
   ISBN 0-7868-6490-7
   1. Barbecue cookery.   I. Schwartz, Joan.   II. Title.
  III. Title: Boy meets grill.
  TX840.B3F54   1999
  641.5'784—dc21   98–45808
                                        CIP

B&N Edition ISBN: 1-4013-0365-X
          ISBN-13: 978-1-4013-0365-5
This edition specially produced for Barnes & Noble by Hyperion.

Design by Joel Avirom and Jason Snyder
Design Assistant: Meghan Day Healey

For my daughter, Sophie:
Every thought I have,
every move I make,
has you in mind.
Love, Daddy
B.F.

For Allen:
From here,
thirty-four years.
J.S.

ACKNOWLEDGMENTS

Thanks to:

My mom, **Dorothy Flay**, for my first Easy Bake™ oven.

My father, **Bill Flay**, for pointing me toward the restaurant business.

Laurence Kretchmer, great friend and business partner, who puts up with my every whim.

Jerry Kretchmer and **Jeff Bliss**, who let me explore whatever I want, whether it's right or wrong.

Stephanie Banyas, who dedicated what seemed like her every moment to making sure this book was completed. Without your expertise and integrity, *Boy Meets Grill* would merely be an idea!

Joan Schwartz, my coauthor, whose tireless dedication to this book went well beyond what anyone could ever ask for. You're the greatest!

Chris Hewitt, former sous chef at Mesa Grill, for his help with the project.

Lisa Dean, whose fun, hip ideas became part of this book.

Maureen O'Brien, editor. It doesn't get to be more fun than this!

Tom Eckerle and **Cece Gallini**, for more beautiful photos and uncompromising style.

Jane Dystel, the best deal maker in publishing.

Patrick O'Brien, for his "Super Bowl" grilling.

My dedicated staffs at Mesa Grill and Bolo, especially: *In the kitchens:* **Wayne Brachman**, **Larry Manheim**, **Erika Lutzner**, and **Bob Mundell**.

In the dining rooms: **Craig Petroff**, **Rick Pitcher**, **J. P. Francois**, **Denise Feltham**, and **Jody Gray**.

Behind the scenes: **Manny Gatdula** and **Stacy Dempsey**.

Special thanks to **Randy Rummel** and **Dynamic Cooking Systems**, for the grill that made these recipes possible, to **Global Knives** for the knives used in the photos, and to **Moss** and **Swid-Powell** for all tabletop props.

PREFACE

My first memories of grilling go back to when I was four or five years old and my mom and dad would rent a house from Memorial Day to Labor Day in Sea Girt, a beautiful small town on the New Jersey shore. Most of my summer diet consisted of "boardwalk food"—hot dogs, hamburgers, and lots of candy. But my favorite meals were when we would break out the grill in the backyard: big lobsters, sweet corn, and, of course, more burgers. The only difficult task was trying to keep the raccoons away after we went to sleep. Lobster shells and corn cobs were their favorite banquet.

I can still remember what those meals tasted like. They were not perfect, but I remember them as delicious and, most important, lots of fun.

For the most part, grilling has always been the focal point of the restaurants that I have worked in or owned. I remember one particular Saturday night at a restaurant named Bud's when we had about 250 reservations and I was working the grill station. We used only mesquite wood, and the grill had to be tended for six hours during dinner service. (You can imagine how much wood we would go through in an evening.) The most crucial part of the night was getting the grill started, not an easy task. It generally took about an hour to get a good hot fire going so that everything—chicken, meats, game, fish, and vegetables—could be cooked to perfection. It was important to know the "hot spots" and "cold spots," and to have a certain command of the grill so that you worked *it*, as opposed to its working *you*.

With all this in mind, I waited for my first orders to come spilling in, and as they did, I suddenly realized that my greatest nightmare had come true. I had forgotten to light the grill! What happened over the next few hours is indescribable, but I think that night has something to do with my preference for gas grills. Press a few buttons, turn a few knobs, and you have a hot, even grill, ready to go.

Today, grilling continues to be much more than a way to cook—it's a whole culture all its own. There's no better way to spend an afternoon for lunch, or a warm evening for a casual dinner. It seems that at every barbecue, at least one person has "the best recipe for this," or "the best way to cook that." Grilling techniques, dry rubs, and marinades have been passed down through generations, and, of course, the best way to fire up a grill always makes for an amusing conversation.

My daughter, Sophie, at a very young age, already has an appreciation for all good things grilled. She must have some of her dad's food genes, because Sophie has been seen running around many backyard barbecues, double-fisted, with grilled lobster and corn niblets in her teeth.

Grilling is a universal word that means something to everyone. Grilling means good times, good friends, and, hopefully, great food. As my good friend Jack McDavid likes to say, "Once you learn how to grill, it's real easy to chill."

—BOBBY FLAY
NEW YORK CITY

CONTENTS

BOBBY FLAY'S
BOY MEETS
GRILL

1. A BOY'S INTRODUCTION TO THE GRILL

Just mention grilling and the first thing I think of is hamburgers. There's absolutely nothing better than a great burger on the grill, seared dark brown and dripping savory juices, covered with melted cheese and grilled sweet onions. I like them a little more well done than most things I grill—probably because I loved those blackened hamburgers I ate at cookouts when I was a kid.

Grilling has always appealed to the "boy" in me, and there's no way I would abandon the classic burgers I remember. But my menu has grown, and I like to slip in the unexpected, as well: clams or mussels steamed in a kettle set on the rack; an entire paella made on the grill; or a table filled with mountains of seared, golden vegetables. I still love to grill simple food, but I add a jolt of bold flavors with seasonings, marinades, and sauces.

I do most of my outdoor cooking during the relaxed weekends I spend on Long Island. The beach, golf, and grilling make up my ritual—they are what life in the summer is all about. I love hitting the farmers' markets, picking up whatever is ripe and fresh, going home, and throwing it on the fire. The great thing is that you can get all this food at the peak of perfection and cook it immediately. I grill dinner almost every night that I'm out there, and often a simple lunch, too, like softshell crabs that I turn into a fabulous sandwich.

My little daughter, Sophie, follows after me, usually with a bag of potato chips in her hand. She likes to help, or at least to hang around while I'm cooking her favorite foods—grilled onions, corn, and lobster.

1

With great ingredients tempting me on all sides, everything I put together on the grill works. In addition, I accumulate interesting spices and flavorings over the season and use them as the spirit moves me. By the time the summer is in full swing, my pantry will contain, in addition to pepper and kosher salt:

- vinegars, such as sherry, balsamic, rice wine, and red wine

- olive oil (I seldom use extra virgin; most of my recipes call for "olive oil," the stuff that used to be called "pure olive oil")

- chile powders such as ancho, pasilla, chile de arbol, and cascabel

- assorted mustards

- cumin

- cilantro

- paprika

- curry powder

One thing I don't use is dried herbs—to me, they all taste like tea. (The only exception is in dry rubs, for crusting steaks or turkey.) Nothing beats fresh herbs, and they are easy to find at most greengrocers and even at supermarkets.

I also make a few stocks the day I plan to cook with them, or else I keep them in the freezer, to be defrosted when needed. Chicken Stock enriches the Sherry Vinegar–Brown Sugar Barbecue Baste for chicken, the Honey Mustard Pan Juice for porterhouse steak, and the Charred Corn Polenta; Shrimp Stock adds flavor to Peanut Dipping Sauce for shrimp; and Vegetable Stock is the base for Grilled Asparagus Risotto. Recipes for these stocks appear at the end of this chapter.

FUNDAMENTALS OF THE FIRE

Don't be intimidated by the grill! It is a source of heat, just like a stove, and very user friendly.

Grilling simply means cooking food quickly over a very hot fire. The food develops a seared, flavorful crust and a juicy interior, but you have to start out with tender meat, fish, or vegetables for this method to work. Grilling differs from barbecuing, which is slow cooking over a lower fire and is suitable for less tender foods.

I'm devoted to my gas grill, but sometimes I also cook with charcoal, and there are a few things to remember in order to do it well. First, hardwood lump charcoal is considered to be better than the more easily available briquettes, because it burns hotter and cleaner. Use plenty of charcoal and light it with an electric coil starter or a chimney starter. The latter device is an open-ended cylinder into which you put crumpled newspaper, top it with charcoal, and light the newspaper. When the charcoal becomes hot, you pour it onto the grill and add additional charcoal on top. There also is a kettle grill that lights the charcoal using gas ignition.

A two-level fire is recommended for cooking flexibility, and this can be constructed in different ways. Either light two piles of charcoal, one larger and one smaller; or light a large pile and after it is hot, move some of the coals off into a smaller pile.

Some of my recipes require high heat, some medium high, and a few require low heat. If you aren't using a gas grill, which has a temperature gauge, measuring the temperature can be a little tricky. The tried and true way is to place your hand an inch or two above the hot charcoal. If you can keep it there for up to two seconds, the fire is hot; three to four seconds means medium hot, five to six indicates medium low to low.

There is some controversy over whether it is better to cook with the grill lid closed or open. Advocates of charcoal grilling seem to prefer the flavor of uncovered food; gas-grill enthusiasts hold that food cooks more evenly and heat is retained better when the cover is down. As with most aspects of

3

grilling, this comes down to personal taste. I always keep the cover down when I am preheating the grill, and I leave it that way through most of the cooking process, as well—otherwise the heat escapes. My general rule is, cook with the grill closed for anything that takes more than four minutes. I close the lid even for most of the quicker things.

When people put something down on the grill, the tendency is to start moving it around immediately, so it won't stick. Actually, the opposite happens: if you move it too soon, it's bound to stick. When you put a piece of food on the grate, let it sit a couple of minutes so it starts to get a seared surface and grill marks. Then move it, if you have to—the seared crust will protect it.

Food cooks quickly on the grill, and it's not difficult to measure doneness. I prefer to decide by appearance, and each recipe will tell you what to look for when you pull the food off the rack. It's a good idea to check while it is cooking, as well, by prodding it a little to judge its firmness (remember how it felt before you put it on the fire, and how it usually feels when it is sitting on your plate); or by cutting into it to see if the inside looks done. The United States Department of Agriculture is more specific and if you want to follow their rules, you will need an instant-read thermometer.

CHOOSING A GRILL

The first choice you make about buying a grill is charcoal or gas. (Electric grills, both outdoor and indoor, don't have the heat you need to grill well, so they aren't an option.) Both can give excellent results, so choose the one that best suits your style of cooking. Gas grills fire up much faster than charcoal, which is one reason I like them so much. My feeling is, now that we have the technology, we might as well use it, but that's strictly personal.

The purist considers only charcoal grilling to be the real thing. There is a whole ritual about choosing the best charcoal, laying the fire and lighting it, and moving food around from hotter to cooler cooking areas. Charcoal provides an extremely hot fire, but it can be difficult to get lit, and then it takes about a half hour to reach cooking temperature, when it becomes covered

4

with a film of gray ash. It can be hard to control the heat, to keep it even. True, charcoal does impart a certain distinctive flavor, although I find the real flavor boost comes from marinades and seasonings, and from quick searing directly over a very hot fire—which a good gas grill does as well as charcoal.

If charcoal is your choice, you will find even the top grills are reasonably priced. Look for a sturdy grill with a cover and a large grilling surface, and, if possible, an adjustable grate and firebox. Weber kettle grills are among the most popular.

A powerful gas grill provides strong heat and is far easier to light—just turn it on. It gives consistent temperatures, whether your food requires low heat or high, and temperature can be adjusted any time during cooking, so you don't have to move the food around. Because gas grills are easy to ignite and they get hot fast, you can spend your time preparing the food, not working on the fire— that's what I like to do. The simple start-up allows for real spontaneity: ten minutes after you make the decision to grill, you can throw the food on the fire.

When shopping for a gas grill, look for one that heats up fast and is sturdy. A porcelain-coated grate will keep the food from sticking—the food comes away from the grill, and that's half the battle. The heat source may be lava rocks, ceramic briquettes, or metal plates or triangles. All are good, but the rocks and briquettes may need occasional cleaning and sometimes replacement. Some grills offer electric rotisseries and side burners as extra features. Among the popular manufacturers are Weber, Viking, Charbroil, and DCS, which manufactures grills for Williams Sonoma. Gas grills are more expensive than charcoal, starting at several hundred dollars and reaching to the stratosphere.

If open-air grilling, either charcoal or gas, isn't an option, its principles can be applied using indoor equipment. A fireplace is the closest alternative, with the addition of a Tuscan grill, a metal frame that holds a grilling grate. Or you can set an ordinary grill rack on top of some bricks to raise the cooking surface above the flames. Keep the flue wide open, just as you must when you

5

light an ordinary fire. Cooking may take a few minutes longer when you use a fireplace, since the food will not be covered.

Some kitchen ranges come with gas grills, but not all provide enough heat to give good results, so check their specifications carefully. Again, you won't cover this grill, so you may need to cook food a little longer.

Finally, consider using a heavy, ridged cast-iron grill pan, preferably seasoned, on your stovetop. Heat it for five to ten minutes before adding the food. You won't achieve optimum results, but you will reach a version of what we're trying to accomplish.

GRILLING EQUIPMENT

Forget the bells and whistles and keep your equipment simple—too many of the accessories you see hanging from hooks on fancy grills are not good for grilling. I prefer my regular kitchen tools to long-handled implements, which I find clumsy to use: I rely on a good, strong pair of tongs and a sturdy spatula that I'm really comfortable with. Don't forget a few heavy-duty potholders or mitts and a strong wire scraper to keep the grid clean. I would rather test food for doneness as it cooks than bother with a thermometer, but if you want to be extra sure when cooking a piece of meat, go ahead and use one. Grilling baskets and trays for vegetables prevent small pieces of food from falling through the grate, although food sometimes can steam rather than grill on them because there is less surface contact with the fire. For kebobs, I prefer bamboo skewers to the thicker metal ones simply because they leave smaller holes in the food.

A WORD ABOUT QUESADILLAS

Grilled foods and tortillas are a natural match, and one of the best ways to combine the two is in a quesadilla. The traditional quesadilla is a stuffed tortilla, more like a turnover. The tortilla is folded in half, covering its filling, and then fried in lots of hot oil. While the idea of a crisp tortilla shell enclosing a spicy, creamy, or

6

chewy filling appeals to me, a turnover seems kind of a dull way to get there. And you can't heap very much filling on half a tortilla.

That's why my quesadillas are stacked: each one has three tortillas separated by two layers of filling—a sort of club quesadilla. I thought these tortilla sandwiches would be a natural for outdoor cooking, and I was right. Over the fire, the tortillas soften a little, the cheese melts beautifully, and all the flavors in the filling—whether lobster and toasted garlic, prosciutto and mozzarella, or chicken and grilled tomatoes—are heightened by the smokiness of the grill.

TIPS FOR GRILLING BOBBY'S WAY

- **BEFORE GRILLING, LESS IS MORE.** Simplicity is the whole thing in grilling, start to finish, and it's perfectly acceptable just to brush food with olive oil and sprinkle it with salt and pepper before putting it on the fire. Of course, you can play with ingredients a little beforehand too, using spice rubs and marinades, but don't overdo them or they will dominate the taste of the food. Save the real blast of flavor for later.

- **AFTER GRILLING, PULL OUT ALL THE STOPS.** Condiments make the dishes distinctive and more interesting than your nextdoor neighbor's barbecue. Be bold with your own fruit- and vegetable-based ketchups, relishes, and salsas that are spicy, tart, or sweet.

- **DO WHAT WORKS. THE GRILL IS NOT SACRED.** Certain foods, such as lobster and corn, will dry out if they are completely cooked on the grill, and some others, like potatoes, will take too long and throw your whole dinner off schedule. The solution here is to precook some food three-quarters of the way through, set it aside, and then throw it on the grill shortly before serving.

7

The opposite works, too. You may plan to serve fish fillets or steaks, but you'd rather not grill them at the last minute. Can you give them the sear and flavor that only a grill can produce, and still do most of the work ahead of time? Yes, if you sear them on the grill, set them aside, and then finish their cooking in the oven when your guests arrive. This can be done with most fish and meat recipes.

- **USE SQUEEZE BOTTLES.** Pour vinaigrettes into squeeze bottles and store them in the refrigerator. They make for a very organized storage system, but even more important, they allow you to control the amount of dressing you put on your salads and other dishes. And it's fun to decorate your foods with swirls of the vinaigrettes.

- **ORGANIZE! PRIORITIZE!** Organize your tasks: plan a menu, make lists, do the shopping. Decide on priorities—know what you can make ahead, whether it's a day or a couple of hours. Plan what you're going to make first, second, and third, and stay in that order, so that by the time your guests come, you have very little left to do besides grilling.

  When it's time to hit the grill, get everything out in front of you. This is what chefs call *mise en place*: all the food, spices, and tools you're going to need should be within easy reach.

The whole idea of grilling is to be casual and festive, so keep it simple. Even if you love to grill as much as I do, don't get carried away and make too much food. Make sure you have a nice array of things to put out, but don't turn the cooking into a burden.

I don't know of any other style of cooking that so easily lends itself to relaxed good times. A meal that's prepared outdoors on the grill invites everyone to loosen up and enjoy the party. People gather around with their drinks, checking on the food and the fire, helping the chef, or just talking and laughing in anticipation of a great meal. All the food goes out on big platters and guests can simply dig in and help themselves. This is my kind of entertaining—give it a try.

STOCKS

SHRIMP STOCK

MAKES 4 TO 5 CUPS

2 tablespoons olive oil

3 cups shells and tails from raw shrimp

1 large onion, coarsely chopped

1 small carrot, peeled and coarsely chopped

1 celery stalk, coarsely chopped

6 cups water

1 cup white wine

1 medium tomato, chopped,
   or ½ cup canned plum tomatoes

1 bay leaf

In a large saucepan over high heat, heat the oil until almost smoking and cook the shrimp shells and tails, onion, carrot, and celery 5 minutes. Add the water, wine, tomato, and bay leaf. Reduce the heat to medium, partly cover, and simmer 40 minutes. Strain through cheesecloth or a fine strainer. May be refrigerated, covered, up to 2 days, or frozen.

9

VEGETABLE STOCK

MAKES 10 CUPS

4 large carrots, peeled and coarsely chopped

2 large whole heads of garlic, unpeeled

3 onions, coarsely chopped

4 leeks (white and half the green), washed well
    and coarsely chopped

5 stalks celery, coarsely chopped

3 parsnips, peeled and coarsely chopped

6 sprigs thyme

8 sprigs flat-leaf parsley

3 bay leaves

1½ tablespoons peppercorns

4 quarts water

Place all the ingredients in a large stockpot and bring to a boil over medium-high heat. Reduce the heat to medium and simmer for 1 hour.

Strain the stock and discard the vegetables. Return the stock to the stove and continue to cook over medium heat, uncovered, until reduced to 10 cups, about 1 hour. May be refrigerated up to 2 days, or frozen.

Chicken Stock

MAKES ABOUT 2 QUARTS

3 pounds chicken bones
3 medium celery stalks, coarsely chopped
3 medium carrots, peeled and coarsely chopped
1 large white onion, coarsely chopped
10 black peppercorns
1 bay leaf
12 parsley stems
Cold water to cover

Place the ingredients in a large pot over high heat and bring to a boil. Reduce the heat to low and simmer, uncovered, 2 hours, skimming as needed.

Strain through a fine strainer and degrease. Discard the solids. May be refrigerated up to 2 days, or frozen.

11

2. BURGERS, SAUSAGES, AND THEIR ACCOMPANIMENTS

Hamburgers have always been the most basic and accessible of grilled foods, and for many people, they still are what grilling is all about. Why would anyone need a recipe for the original cooking-by-instinct dish? Just get some ground meat and throw it on the grill—even a rank amateur can't mess up with that.

I don't want to complicate something so beautifully simple, but I have a few things to add.

Quality ingredients and a little care in cooking will make the difference between a spectacular burger and one that is only passable, or maybe even bland and dried out. Get fresh coarsely ground chuck (extra lean cuts won't make a tastier burger) and use it as soon as you can after purchase. Form it into somewhat loose patties and season them with salt and pepper.

Turn the gas grill to high or prepare a hot charcoal fire and sear the burgers to seal in the juices and get those appetizing dark-brown grill marks. Cook about 4 minutes on each side, with the cover closed, for medium rare; 5 for medium; and 6 for well done.

Buffalo, which is low in fat and has an intense beefy flavor, also makes an excellent hamburger, especially with slices of goat cheese melted over the top. Because it has less fat than beef, be extra careful to watch it so it doesn't overcook and dry out.

There is a whole world of burgers out there, and only some of them are made from red meat. I especially like a terrific turkey burger that has a molten center of melted Brie. The cheese adds moisture to the ground turkey, which tends to be dry, and enriches its flavor. And it makes for a nice surprise when you take a bite. Good-quality ground turkey is easy to find at your butcher or supermarket, or you can grind your own in the food processor, customizing the proportions of light and dark meat.

Tuna makes a hearty, chewy burger and rumor has it that it's kind to the cholesterol level. Make sure the fish is perfectly fresh and keep it cold, so it holds together when you form the burgers. Mince it very fine with a sharp knife, not in a food processor, which will turn it to mush. I find tuna burgers take well to a sweet and spicy glaze of pineapple and mustard. Delicious!

Italian sausage is another kind of ground meat that's sensational on the grill. Nothing brings out its sweet fennel flavor or peppery spiciness like cooking over a hot fire; it comes off crisp and smoky and ready to be paired with sweet and tart Grilled Onion Marmalade and deliciously charred Grilled Bell Peppers. A crowd pleaser every time.

The accompaniments are what really make burgers and sausages soar. Your Roasted Tomato Ketchup will be miles ahead of the bottled red stuff, with the freshness of ripe tomatoes, plus its own uniquely smoky notes, and the garlic bread you make with Roasted Garlic Butter will have a crisp-toasted grilled surface. Homemade Grilled Onion Marmalade, Spicy Cucumber Pickles, and Red Chile–Dusted Potato Chips are all easy to make and round out any menu.

You will find all these accompaniments listed in chapter 2, and many others throughout this and other chapters, as part of specific recipes. They all can be mixed and matched according to your own taste and the current bounty of the farmers' market. For instance, try your tuna burgers with the Fig and Nectarine Relish that goes so well with grilled tuna; serve turkey burgers with the Yellow Tomato–Roasted Garlic Salsa that you normally make with a Grilled

Lobster Quesadilla; or accompany your buffalo burger with Basil-Marinated Tomatoes, from the porterhouse steak recipe. Instead of the Grilled Onion Marmalade on your sausage sandwich, try the Grilled Pineapple Relish I give you with Spicy Pineapple-Glazed Sea Scallops, or the Apricot Chutney that goes with the Moroccan Spice–Rubbed Leg of Lamb.

Flatbreads are pizza by another name, and they make terrific partners to any grilled dish—or outstanding meals on their own. As long as your grill is hot enough and you have your dough made ahead of time, all you do is roll out the dough, brush with a little olive oil, add your topping, and grill. The list of possibilities is basically endless.

RECIPES

Hamburgers with Double Cheddar Cheese, Grilled Vidalia Onions, and Horseradish Mustard

Turkey Burgers Filled with Brie and Grilled Granny Smith Apple Slices

Buffalo Burgers with Goat Cheese, Mango Ketchup, and Red Slaw

Tuna Burgers with Pineapple-Mustard Glaze and Green Chile–Pickle Relish

Grilled Italian Sausage Sandwiches with Grilled Onion Marmalade and Grilled Bell Peppers

ACCOMPANIMENTS

Spicy Cucumber Pickles

Red Chile–Dusted Potato Chips

Grilled Bread with Roasted Garlic Butter and Fresh Herbs

Mesa Barbecue Sauce

Roasted Tomato Ketchup

Grilled Flatbread

Grilled Flatbread with Caramelized Onions, Cabrales Blue Cheese, and Wild Mushrooms

Grilled Flatbread with Garlic-Rubbed Filet of Beef, White Bean Puree, and Sun-Dried Tomato Relish

Grilled Flatbread with Ricotta Cheese, Fresh Tomatoes, Basil, and Roasted Garlic Oil

15

Hamburgers with Double Cheddar Cheese, Grilled Vidalia Onions, and Horseradish Mustard

MAKES 8 SERVINGS

I grew up eating hamburgers at J. G. Melon's, on New York's Upper East Side, where they make the best in the world. I always try to emulate their burgers on the grill, but I really haven't a clue about their secret—just simple, good burgers.

Vidalia onions, grown only in Georgia, are in season from April through October. Raw or cooked, they are sweet as candy, and are delicious grilled with a little olive oil, salt, and pepper.

FOR THE GRILLED VIDALIA ONIONS:

**2 Vidalia onions, sliced crosswise ½ inch thick
(do not separate into rings)
Olive oil for brushing
Kosher salt and freshly ground pepper**

Preheat a gas or charcoal grill to high.

Brush the onions with olive oil on both sides and season with salt and pepper. Grill until golden brown, 3 to 4 minutes on each side.

16

FOR THE HORSERADISH MUSTARD:

1 cup Dijon mustard

2 tablespoons finely grated fresh horseradish, or prepared horseradish, drained

Mix the mustard and horseradish together in a small bowl. May be refrigerated up to 1 week; serve at room temperature. Makes 1 cup.

FOR THE HAMBURGERS:

2½ pounds freshly ground chuck (slightly coarse grind)
Kosher salt and freshly ground pepper
Sixteen ¼-inch-thick slices Cheddar cheese
8 hamburger buns
8 leaves romaine lettuce
Grilled Vidalia Onions
Eight ¼-inch-thick slices beefsteak tomato (2 tomatoes)
Horseradish Mustard

Divide the chuck into eight 5-ounce burgers and season on both sides with salt and pepper (handle as little as possible and form the burgers loosely). On the preheated grill, cook 3 to 4 minutes on each side for medium rare.

During the last minutes of cooking, top each burger with 2 slices of cheese, cover the grill, and let the cheese melt, about 1 minute. Split the buns and toast on the grill, cut side down, until golden.

Place a burger in each bun and top with lettuce, onions, tomato, and a dollop of Horseradish Mustard. Arrange on a large platter.

17

Turkey Burgers Filled with Brie and Grilled Granny Smith Apple Slices

MAKES 8 SERVINGS

Turkey burgers have been around for a while but I'd never tried one before I made some on my television show, *The Main Ingredient*. Then I really fell in love with them! Playing with the original recipe, I added the surprise of melted Brie in the middle, for richness and moisture. The grilled Granny Smith apples that top the burgers are delicious, even as a snack—just ask my daughter, Sophie.

2½ pounds ground turkey

Eight ½-inch cubes of Brie cheese

Olive oil for brushing the turkey burgers

Kosher salt and freshly ground pepper

2 large Granny Smith apples,
    cored and sliced ½ inch crosswise

2 tablespoons vegetable oil

2 loaves of French or Italian bread,
    cut crosswise into quarters

2 cups arugula

Preheat a gas or charcoal grill to high.

Shape the ground turkey into 8 round patties about 1½ inches thick. Make a small indentation in the center of each patty, place 1 cube of cheese in it, and press the turkey up and around, to cover it. Brush both sides of the burger lightly with the olive oil and season with salt and pepper.

Grill until cooked through, about 4 minutes on each side.

While the burgers are cooking, brush the apples on both sides with vegetable oil and grill until golden, about 2 minutes on each side.

Split the bread and toast on the grill, cut side down, until golden. Place a burger on the bottom of each quarter. Top with 1 or 2 apple slices, several sprigs of arugula, and the remaining bread. Arrange the burgers on a large platter.

19

Buffalo Burgers with Goat Cheese, Mango Ketchup, and Red Slaw

MAKES 8 SERVINGS

Mesa Grill has become buffalo country with these burgers, as well as a popular sandwich of roasted brisket. Buffalo is low in fat and has a clean beef flavor, and because it is farm raised, it isn't at all gamey.

Allen Susser of Chef Allen's restaurant in Miami makes and bottles terrific Mango Ketchup™, which inspired me to play with the flavors of ripe fruit and spices and to come up with my own version, different, but good. You can make mine or buy his.

FOR THE MANGO KETCHUP:

> 2 tablespoons olive oil
> 1 small onion, coarsely chopped
> 2 cloves garlic, coarsely chopped
> ¼ teaspoon cinnamon
> ¼ teaspoon allspice
> 1 tablespoon honey
> Pinch of cloves
> 1 small habañero pepper, seeded and finely chopped
> 1 ripe mango, peeled, pitted, and coarsely chopped
> 1 teaspoon Dijon mustard
> ¼ cup red wine vinegar
> Kosher salt and freshly ground pepper

Heat the olive oil in a medium saucepan over medium heat. Add the onion and garlic and cook until soft. Add the cinnamon, allspice, honey, cloves, and habañero pepper, and cook an additional 1 minute. Add the mango and continue cooking until softened, 15 to 20 minutes.

20

Place the mango mixture in the bowl of a food processor, add the mustard and vinegar, and process until smooth. Season with salt and pepper to taste. May be refrigerated for 1 day; serve at room temperature. Makes about 2 cups.

FOR THE RED SLAW:

1 large head red cabbage, finely shredded

3 cups red wine vinegar

1 tablespoon honey

3 tablespoons olive oil

Kosher salt and freshly ground pepper

2 tablespoons poppy seeds

Place the cabbage in a large bowl. Place the vinegar in a saucepan and bring to a simmer over medium heat. Remove from the heat, add the honey and oil, and mix well. Pour the mixture over the cabbage, stir to combine, and season with salt, pepper, and poppy seeds. Cover with plastic wrap and let sit for 30 minutes. May be refrigerated for 1 day; serve at room temperature.

FOR THE BUFFALO BURGERS:

2½ pounds buffalo meat, finely ground

16 slices of soft goat cheese

Olive oil for brushing the burgers

Kosher salt and freshly ground pepper

8 hamburger buns

Preheat a gas or charcoal grill to high.

Shape the meat into 8 burgers, brush with olive oil, and season with salt and pepper. Grill 3 to 4 minutes on each side for medium rare. (Don't overcook, because the longer you cook, the less juicy they well be.) About 30 seconds before the burgers are done, top each with 2 slices of goat cheese and close the cover to melt the cheese. Split the buns and toast on the grill, cut side down, until golden. Serve on buns, topped with Mango Ketchup and Red Slaw.

21

Tuna Burgers with Pineapple-Mustard Glaze and Green Chile-Pickle Relish

MAKES 8 SERVINGS

When you don't want to eat red meat, tuna makes a satisfying burger, with its robust flavor and texture. It provides a good canvas for Asian spices, and this recipe is a terrific way to play with Asian ingredients. When you buy a large tuna steak, save the ends to use the next day for burgers.

You have to chop tuna by hand, so it is minced fine. Never chop it in a food processor! Make sure it is very fresh and very cold.

FOR THE PINEAPPLE-MUSTARD GLAZE:

3 cups pineapple juice

1 cup white wine vinegar

2 tablespoons soy sauce

1 teaspoon peeled and finely chopped gingerroot

¼ cup light brown sugar, firmly packed

2 tablespoons Dijon mustard

3 tablespoons fresh lime juice

1 teaspoon freshly ground white pepper

In a small saucepan over high heat, combine the pineapple juice, vinegar, soy sauce, gingerroot, and brown sugar, and bring to a boil. Cook until the volume is reduced by half, stirring occasionally, about 30 minutes. Add the mustard and cook an additional 2 minutes. Remove from the heat and add the lime juice and pepper. Let cool at room temperature. May be refrigerated for 1 day; use at room temperature. Makes about 2 cups.

22

FOR THE GREEN CHILE–PICKLE RELISH:

4 poblano peppers, grilled, peeled, seeded,
    and finely diced (see Note)
3 medium dill pickles, finely diced
¼ cup finely diced red onion
3 tablespoons fresh lime juice
1 tablespoon honey
2 tablespoons finely chopped cilantro
Kosher salt and freshly ground pepper

Combine the poblanos, pickles, onion, lime juice, honey, and cilantro in a medium bowl and season with salt and pepper. Let sit at room temperature 30 minutes before serving. May be refrigerated, covered, for 1 day; serve at room temperature. Makes about 3 cups.

FOR THE TUNA BURGERS:

2½ pounds tuna steak, finely chopped by hand
Kosher salt and freshly ground pepper
8 pumpernickel rolls
2 cups watercress

Shape the ground tuna into 8 round patties about 1½ inches thick and refrigerate, covered, 30 minutes or up to overnight. (The burgers must be very cold to hold their shape while cooking.)

Preheat a gas or charcoal grill to high. Season the burgers on both sides with salt and pepper and grill 3 to 4 minutes for medium. Remove and brush on one side with the Pineapple-Mustard Glaze. Split the rolls and toast on the grill. Place each burger in a roll and top with Green Chile–Pickle Relish and watercress. Serve on a large platter.

NOTE: To grill poblanos, brush with olive oil and season with salt and pepper. Grill over high heat until charred on all sides. Place in a bowl, cover with plastic wrap, and let sit for 15 minutes. Then peel, halve, and seed.

23

BURGERS, SAUSAGES, AND THEIR ACCOMPANIMENTS

BOY MEETS GRILL

Grilled Italian Sausage Sandwiches with Grilled Onion Marmalade and Grilled Bell Peppers

MAKES 8 SERVINGS

One whiff of these sausages sizzling on the grill, and I'm transported to New York City's San Gennaro Festival, where wonderful Italian cooking is done outdoors on the city streets and the air is filled with peppery aromas. People go from one food stand to another and the parade of delicious food never stops.

FOR THE GRILLED ONION MARMALADE:

3 red onions, halved

2 tablespoons olive oil, plus extra for brushing the onions

Kosher salt and freshly ground pepper

2 cloves garlic, finely chopped

1 small jalapeño pepper

1 cup red wine vinegar

¼ cup crème de cassis

¼ cup grenadine

¼ cup red wine

¼ cup chopped parsley

Preheat a gas or charcoal grill to high.

Brush the onions with olive oil, season with salt and pepper, and grill until lightly browned on both sides and cooked through, 3 to 4 minutes. Remove from the grill and slice thin.

Heat the remaining olive oil until almost smoking in a medium saucepan over medium heat, or on the grill. Add the onions, garlic, and jalapeño and cook for 1 minute. Add the vinegar, crème de cassis, grenadine, and red wine, and cook until reduced almost to dry. Remove from the heat, add the parsley, and season with salt and pepper. May be refrigerated for 1 day; serve at room temperature. Makes about 2 cups.

FOR THE SAUSAGE SANDWICHES:

3 red bell peppers, grilled, seeded, and cut into eighths (see Note)
1½ pounds hot Italian sausage links, halved lengthwise
1½ pounds sweet Italian sausage links
8 hoagie or hero rolls (individual Italian sandwich loaves)
Grilled Onion Marmalade
Dijon mustard

Preheat a gas grill to medium high or light a medium-hot charcoal fire.

Grill the sausages, turning, until golden brown and cooked completely through, 15 to 20 minutes. Slice in half lengthwise.

Slice the rolls in half lengthwise and toast on the grill, split-side down, until golden. Fill with sausages, onion marmalade, and bell peppers. Pile the sandwiches on a platter and serve with the mustard on the side.

NOTE: To grill the bell peppers, brush with olive oil and season with salt and pepper. Grill over high heat until charred on all sides. Place in a bowl, cover with plastic wrap, and let sit for 15 minutes. Then peel, halve, and seed.

25

ACCOMPANIMENTS

Spicy Cucumber Pickles

MAKES 4 CUPS

These crisp slices add a tangy crunch to your grilled dishes. Make them once and you'll see that there is no mystery to homemade pickles.

4 cups rice wine vinegar

2 tablespoons sugar

½ teaspoon red pepper flakes

1 teaspoon whole white peppercorns

1 teaspoon coriander seeds

1 teaspoon mustard seeds

½ teaspoon fennel seeds

½ teaspoon toasted cumin seeds (see Note)

1 tablespoon kosher salt

2 tablespoons coarsely chopped fresh dill

2 tablespoons coarsely chopped cilantro

2 unpeeled English cucumbers, washed and sliced crosswise ½ inch thick

Combine the vinegar, sugar, pepper flakes, peppercorns, coriander seeds, mustard seeds, fennel seeds, cumin seeds, and salt in a medium noncorrosive saucepan over high heat and bring to a boil. Let boil for 2 minutes; remove from the heat and let sit until cooled to room temperature. Add the dill and cilantro.

Place the cucumbers in a large bowl and pour the cooled vinegar mixture over them. Refrigerate, covered, for 24 hours or up to 4 days.

NOTE: To toast cumin seeds, place them in a heavy, dry skillet over low heat and cook 1 to 2 minutes, tossing or stirring them so they don't burn. Remove from the heat as soon as they are toasted.

RED CHILE-DUSTED POTATO CHIPS

MAKES 8 CUPS

Ancho chile powder, along with aromatic cumin, gives great flavor and perfume to crisp potato chips, but if you try for a shortcut and toss them with some chips that you've bought, they simply won't work. When the spices hit the crunchy chips just as they come out of the hot oil, you'll see what I mean.

> 4 cups peanut or canola oil
> 4 large potatoes, peeled and sliced ⅛ inch thick
> ½ cup ancho chile powder (see Note)
> 2 tablespoons ground cumin
> Kosher salt

In a large pot or deep fryer, heat the oil to 360°F and fry the chips in several batches until crisp and golden, about 2 minutes. Drain on paper towels. Toss while still hot with the chile powder, cumin, and salt to taste. May be made up to 2 days ahead and stored, covered, at room temperature.

NOTE: Ancho chile powder is available at Hispanic or gourmet markets, or from Kitchen Market, 218 Eighth Avenue, New York, NY 10011, 212-243-4433, which has a mail-order list.

27

Grilled Bread with Roasted Garlic Butter and Fresh Herbs

MAKES 8 SERVINGS

What makes this bread different from others is its roasted garlic flavoring, along with the toasting it gets on the grill. Put it in the middle of the table when you're serving a big grilled feast.

- 1 head roasted garlic, peeled and mashed to a paste (see Note)
- ½ pound (2 sticks) unsalted butter, softened
- Kosher salt and freshly ground pepper
- 16 slices French or Italian bread (¼ inch thick)
- ¼ cup finely chopped parsley
- ¼ cup finely chopped oregano

Preheat a gas or charcoal grill to high.

In a small bowl, combine the garlic and butter and season with salt and pepper. Spread 1 tablespoon butter on one side of each slice of bread and grill, butterside down, until lightly golden. Turn over each slice, sprinkle with parsley and oregano, and grill 20 seconds.

NOTE: To oven-roast a head of garlic, first cut off the top. Rub the garlic with olive oil and sprinkle with salt and pepper, wrap it in foil, place it on a baking sheet, and roast at 300°F until soft, about 45 minutes.

MESA BARBECUE SAUCE

MAKES ABOUT 2 CUPS

At Mesa Grill, this barbecue sauce is used as is, or as a base for some more complex sauces. The ancho and pasilla chile powders add Southwestern flavors to the traditional barbecue-sauce ingredients: tomatoes, onions, garlic, sweet molasses, and brown sugar.

2 tablespoons canola oil

1 medium red onion, finely diced

3 garlic cloves, minced

8 plum tomatoes, seeded and coarsely diced

¼ cup ketchup

½ cup red wine vinegar

1 tablespoon Worcestershire sauce

¼ cup water

3 tablespoons dark molasses

2 tablespoons Dijon mustard

2 tablespoons dark brown sugar

1 tablespoon honey

1 teaspoon cayenne

1 tablespoon ancho chile powder (see Note)

1 tablespoon pasilla chile powder (see Note)

1 tablespoon paprika

Heat the canola oil until almost smoking in a large saucepan over medium heat and sweat the onion and garlic until softened but not colored, about 5 minutes. Add the tomatoes and simmer 15 minutes. Add the remaining ingredients and simmer 20 minutes. Pour the mixture in a food processor and puree.

Pour into a medium bowl and let cool to room temperature. May be refrigerated up to 1 week or frozen.

NOTE: Ancho and pasilla chile powders are available at Hispanic or gourmet markets, or mail order from Kitchen Market, 218 Eighth Avenue, New York, NY 10011, 212-243-4433.

29

ROASTED TOMATO KETCHUP

MAKES ABOUT 2 CUPS

There is no comparison between the stuff that comes in bottles and your own ketchup, made from fresh ripe tomatoes, onions, garlic, and spices—it's not even close. This is a good thing to make with any over-ripe tomatoes you have around.

1½ **pounds ripe tomatoes, cored and quartered**
¼ **cup olive oil**
1 **medium onion, finely diced**
2 **cloves garlic, finely diced**
¼ **cup cider vinegar**
2 **tablespoons brown sugar**
¼ **teaspoon cinnamon**
¼ **teaspoon allspice**
3 **tablespoons honey**
Kosher salt and freshly ground pepper

Preheat the oven to 350°F.

In a small bowl, toss the tomatoes in 2 tablespoons of the olive oil and place on a baking sheet. Roast until soft, 10 to 15 minutes. Transfer the tomatoes to a food processor and process until smooth. Strain, pressing against the solids with a wooden spoon to extract as much pulp and juice as possible.

Heat the remaining 2 tablespoons of olive oil in a medium saucepan over medium heat until almost smoking, and sauté the onion and garlic until translucent. Add the tomato puree, cider vinegar, brown sugar, cinnamon, allspice, and honey, and season with salt and pepper. Continue cooking, uncovered, stirring occasionally, until thick, 25 to 30 minutes. May be refrigerated, covered, up to 2 days.

Grilled Flatbread

MAKES 4 FLATBREADS, SERVING 8

These are unbelievable! Don't be nervous about grilling pizza dough (the foundation of the flatbreads)—it's easy and it works. The grill gives flatbread a golden crust and a deliciously chewy interior, along with a smoky grilled flavor that you can't get any other way. When they hit the fire, the circles or rectangles of dough become asymmetrical and kind of rough-hewn, giving the loaves a beautiful rustic appearance. There are several steps to the process, but if you like, you can grill the pizza dough ahead and assemble the breads later when your guests arrive. If you're really pressed for time, you can even make these breads with purchased pizza dough.

When it's showtime, have all your toppings at hand and quickly put them on the loaves right on the grill. I suggest three and all are great combinations of flavor. The first is earthy, with caramelized onions, Cabrales blue cheese, and sautéed wild mushrooms. The second is robust and filling enough to be a meal, with grilled beef filet over a garlicky white bean purée, covered with a sweet and tart tomato relish. The third is the most classic, with ripe plum tomatoes, ricotta cheese, and basil heaped on the crisp crust. Just about anything you can put on a pizza will make a terrific flatbread, so feel free to improvise.

> 1½ cups warm water
> ½ teaspoon dry yeast
> 4 cups all-purpose flour
> ½ teaspoon salt
> 2 tablespoons olive oil

(continued)

31

Mix the water and yeast in a medium bowl and let stand 15 minutes. Gradually pour in 2 cups of the flour and stir to incorporate. Mix for about 1 minute to form a sponge. Let stand at room temperature, covered, for 45 minutes.

Put the sponge in the bowl of a standing mixer. Using the dough hook, mix in the salt and oil, and add the remaining flour ½ cup at a time, mixing, to form a soft dough. Place the dough on a lightly floured work surface and knead until it is satiny, sprinkling with a little flour to keep it from sticking, about 5 minutes.

Place the dough in a large, clean, oiled bowl, cover with plastic wrap, and let rise in a warm place until doubled, about 2½ hours. Punch down the dough and divide into 4 balls. Place on a sheet pan, cover with plastic wrap, and let rise until almost doubled, 30 to 45 minutes. Roll, pat, and stretch the dough into 4 roughly shaped 10- to 12-inch circles or rectangles. They don't have to look perfect.

When ready to grill, proceed with any of the following recipes.

Grilled Flatbread with Caramelized Onions, Cabrales Blue Cheese, and Wild Mushrooms

MAKES 4 FLATBREADS, SERVING 8

2 tablespoons unsalted butter

½ cup plus 2 tablespoons olive oil

3 medium Spanish onions, thinly sliced

1 teaspoon sugar

2 pounds assorted wild mushrooms (portobello, shiitake, chanterelle, porcini), stemmed and cleaned

Kosher salt and freshly ground pepper

1 pound fresh mozzarella, thinly sliced

Four 10- to 12-inch rounds or rectangles of flatbread dough

1 cup crumbled Cabrales blue cheese

Preheat a gas or charcoal grill to medium or use a side burner (or the stove).

Melt the butter with 2 tablespoons of the olive oil in a large sauté pan. Add the onions and sugar and cook until soft and caramelized, 15 to 20 minutes.

Heat ¼ cup of olive oil in a large sauté pan over high heat and sauté the mushrooms until golden brown and soft. Season with salt and pepper.

Preheat a gas or charcoal grill to medium high. Brush the rounds of dough with the remaining ¼ cup of olive oil and grill until crusty and golden brown on one side, about 4 minutes. Turn over and grill another 4 minutes.

Remove from the grill and place on a sheet of aluminum foil. Spread each bread with the mozzarella, onions, and mushrooms, and sprinkle with the crumbled blue cheese. Close the grill cover and cook for 3 minutes.

Place the breads on a large platter and cut into quarters.

33

Grilled Flatbread with Garlic-Rubbed Filet of Beef, White Bean Puree, and Sun-Dried Tomato Relish

MAKES 4 FLATBREADS, SERVING 8

FOR THE WHITE BEAN PUREE:

2 cups cooked or canned white beans, drained

4 cloves garlic, smashed and peeled

3 tablespoons olive oil

2 tablespoons lemon juice

1 tablespoon chopped thyme

Kosher salt and freshly ground pepper

Puree the beans, garlic, olive oil, lemon juice, and thyme in a food processor. Season with salt and pepper. May be refrigerated for 1 day. Makes 2 cups.

FOR THE SUN-DRIED TOMATO RELISH:

8 sun-dried tomatoes in oil, drained and julienned (cut into thin matchsticks)

4 roasted shallots, sliced thin (see Note)

2 tablespoons olive oil

1 tablespoon balsamic vinegar

1 teaspoon honey

Kosher salt and freshly ground pepper

In a small bowl, mix together the tomatoes, shallots, olive oil, balsamic vinegar, and honey. Season with salt and pepper. May be refrigerated for 1 day; serve at room temperature. Makes about 1 cup.

FOR THE FILET OF BEEF:

> ½ cup olive oil
> 1 head garlic, cloves smashed and peeled
> 1 pound beef tenderloin

Combine the olive oil and garlic and pour over the beef in a shallow pan or baking dish. Refrigerate, covered, 4 hours or overnight, turning once.

Preheat a gas or charcoal grill to high. Remove the beef from the oil, shaking off any excess (discard the used oil). Grill the beef, turning, 8 minutes total for medium rare. Let rest 10 minutes and slice thinly.

FOR THE FLATBREAD:

> Four 10- to 12-inch rounds or rectangles of flatbread dough
> Olive oil for brushing the dough
> White Bean Puree
> Sliced Filet of Beef
> Sun-Dried Tomato Relish

Preheat a gas or charcoal grill to medium-high. Brush the rounds of dough liberally with olive oil and grill until crusty and golden brown on one side, about 4 minutes. Turn over and grill another 4 minutes.

Remove from the grill and place on a sheet of aluminum foil. Spread each bread with a thin layer of the white bean puree, sliced beef, and tomato relish. Close the grill cover and cook for 3 minutes.

Place the breads on a large platter and cut into quarters.

NOTE: To roast shallots, rub with olive oil, sprinkle with salt and pepper, and place on a sheet pan in a preheated 300°F oven. Roast for 45 minutes. When the shallots are done, their skins will slip off easily.

35

Grilled Flatbread with Ricotta Cheese, Fresh Tomatoes, Basil, and Roasted Garlic Oil

MAKES 4 FLATBREADS, SERVING 8

FOR THE ROASTED GARLIC OIL:

½ cup olive oil
6 cloves roasted garlic, peeled (see Note 1)

Place the oil and garlic in a blender and blend until smooth. Strain and pour into a squeeze bottle. May be refrigerated, covered, for 1 day; use at room temperature. Makes about ½ cup.

FOR THE FLATBREAD:

Four 10- to 12-inch rounds or rectangles of flatbread dough
Olive oil for brushing the dough
1 pound mozzarella, thinly sliced
3 plum tomatoes, diced
¼ cup basil, chiffonade (see Note 2)
1 pound ricotta cheese, drained (see Note 3)
Shaved Parmesan, for garnish

Preheat a gas or charcoal grill to medium high.

Brush the rounds of dough liberally with olive oil and grill until crusty and golden brown on one side, about 4 minutes. Turn over and grill another 4 minutes.

Remove from the grill and place on a sheet of aluminum foil. Spread each bread with the mozzarella, tomatoes, and basil. Place tablespoons of the ricotta around the edge of the bread. Close the grill cover and cook for 3 minutes.

Place the breads on a large platter and drizzle with the Roasted Garlic Oil. Garnish with shaved Parmesan. Cut into quarters.

NOTES:

1. To oven-roast a head of garlic, first cut off the top. Rub the garlic with olive oil and sprinkle with salt and pepper, wrap it in foil, place it on a baking sheet, and roast at 300°F until soft, about 45 minutes.

2. To cut basil into chiffonade, or fine ribbons, roll up the leaves and cut into thin strips.

3. To drain ricotta cheese, place it in a cheesecloth-lined strainer over a bowl for 1 hour. Discard the liquid that remains in the bowl.

37

3. CHICKEN AND OTHER POULTRY

Chicken makes a great canvas for a lot of different flavors, whether from marinades, glazes brushed on over the fire, or sauces, salsas, and relishes—it holds on to all of them. Indonesian-style chicken breasts are bathed in olive oil, citrus juices, ginger, garlic, chiles, cilantro, and honey and then are cooled by a yogurt sauce that echoes many of the same notes. A Jamaican-influenced marinade combining the hottest of peppers with sweet spices, fresh herbs, fresh gingerroot, and lime juice flavors chicken thighs and legs that are then accompanied by a juicy Mango-Cilantro Relish. A Mediterranean mixture of lemon, garlic and basil, and an American Sherry Vinegar–Brown Sugar Barbecue Baste give depth to whole butterflied chickens. Can these grilled birds ever be dull? Not in my backyard.

When you're grilling a whole chicken, butterflying is the way to go. Splitting the chicken down the back and flattening it slightly makes it nice and even, so that it cooks consistently and quickly. Most of the time, though, chicken parts are the easiest to do on the grill. If you cook them with the skin off, they may not have the crispiness of chicken with the skin on, but they still will have appetizing grill marks and a smoky flavor. A marinade or glaze will give the surface a glistening, caramelized color, as well as a spicy kick. Chunks of skinless chicken are ideal for skewering, especially when brushed and basted with a tart-sweet barbecue sauce.

Chicken with the skin on can be tricky to grill consistently. Over high heat, the skin can burn or become marked by the grill, but still remain fatty. In addition, the sugar in barbecue sauces or glazes burns before the meat has cooked through. The solution is to cook the chicken over lower heat, skin-side down, and let the fat render and the skin become golden brown and crisp. Once you get the hang of it, you will be able to grill your chicken so it comes out crisp and juicy in the right places.

The same holds true for duck breasts, which can be very impressive on the grill when done properly. Cook them at low heat or on the cooler part of the grate, to render their considerable fat and to get the skin crisp. The low heat also allows you to coat them with the sensational Plum-Ginger Glaze, which adds spicy Asian flavors. A whole duck has so much fat, I find the only way to grill it successfully is on a spit or rotisserie. This may be a little high tech, but it makes a magnificent duck, laquered in Asian fashion.

Turkey breasts take to a marinade of many flavors and are cooked as easily as chicken breasts. And for a real surprise, try grilling turkey breasts cut into "porterhouse steaks" in the style of grill expert Jack McDavid.

RECIPES

BUTTERFLIED CHICKEN WITH LEMON, GARLIC, AND BASIL

BUTTERFLIED CHICKEN WITH SHERRY VINEGAR—BROWN SUGAR BARBECUE BASTE

GRILLED CHICKEN COBB SALAD WITH SMOKED CHILE—BUTTERMILK DRESSING

RED CHILE—CITRUS MARINATED CHICKEN BREASTS WITH GRILLED TORTILLAS AND AVOCADO-TOMATILLO SALSA

RED-HOT MARINATED CHICKEN SKEWERS WITH YOGURT-CILANTRO SAUCE

BARBECUED CHICKEN QUESADILLAS WITH GRILLED TOMATO SALSA AND BUTTERMILK DRESSING

LARRY'S TANGERINE-GLAZED CHICKEN SKEWERS

INDONESIAN-STYLE CHICKEN WITH GREEN ONION—YOGURT SAUCE

JERKED CHICKEN WITH MANGO-CILANTRO RELISH AND BARBECUED RED ONIONS

DUCK BREASTS WITH FRESH PLUM-GINGER GLAZE AND TOMATILLO RELISH

SPIT-ROASTED DUCK LACQUERED WITH SPICY ORANGE GLAZE

JACK'S TURKEY PORTERHOUSE STEAKS

TURKEY BREAST MARINATED IN MOLASSES, ORANGE, GINGER, AND GARLIC WITH ORANGE-POMEGRANATE RELISH

40

Butterflied Chicken
with Lemon, Garlic, and Basil

MAKES 8 SERVINGS

My friend Paul del Favero, former chef at Nick and Toni's in the Hamptons, always made great butterflied baby chicken, which inspired me to create this recipe. Butterflying makes the chicken nice and even, giving it uniform thickness, so it is easy to grill. The lemon, garlic, and basil flavors make it summery and light.

1 cup olive oil

8 cloves garlic, coarsely chopped

½ cup fresh lemon juice (2 to 3 lemons)

4 chickens (2½ pounds each), butterflied (see Note)

8 lemon slices

32 basil leaves

Kosher salt and freshly ground pepper

Mix together the olive oil, garlic, and lemon juice in a large shallow pan or baking dish. Add the chickens and turn to coat. Cover and marinate in the refrigerator for at least 2 hours or up to 4 hours.

Preheat a gas or charcoal grill to medium high.

Remove each chicken from the marinade and shake off any excess (discard the used marinade). Loosen the skin around the breast and place 1 lemon slice and 4 basil leaves on the breast. Stretch the skin over them, and secure with toothpicks, if too loose. Season the chickens with salt and pepper.

Grill skin-side down until golden brown, 4 to 5 minutes. Turn over and continue grilling until cooked through, turning occasionally, 15 to 20 minutes.

Place on a large serving platter.

NOTE: To butterfly a chicken, split it down the backbone and open it out flat.

41

Butterflied Chicken with Sherry Vinegar–Brown Sugar Barbecue Baste

MAKES 8 SERVINGS

You have to tend this chicken—keep spooning or brushing the barbecue baste over it as it cooks—so the sugar in the baste caramelizes but doesn't burn. Enlist your guests to help. You want somebody standing there the whole time to keep on basting, making sure the sweet crust is forming. As in the previous recipe, butterflying chicken helps it cook evenly.

FOR THE BARBECUE BASTE:

> 2 tablespoons olive oil
>
> 2 shallots, coarsely chopped
>
> 4 cloves garlic, coarsely chopped
>
> 1 cup sherry vinegar
>
> ¼ cup dark brown sugar
>
> 6 plum tomatoes, coarsely chopped
>
> 1½ cups homemade Chicken Stock (page 11),
>   or low-sodium canned
>
> 1 tablespoon Spanish paprika
>
> Kosher salt and freshly ground pepper

Preheat a gas or charcoal grill to medium high or use a side burner (or a stove).

Heat the olive oil in a medium saucepan over medium-high heat until almost smoking and cook the shallots and garlic until soft, 4 to 5 minutes. Add the vinegar and reduce by half. Add the brown sugar, tomatoes, stock, and paprika; stir, and bring to a boil. Reduce the heat to medium and simmer for 20 minutes. Transfer the

42

mixture to a food processor and process until smooth. Return the mixture to a clean medium saucepan and cook over low heat until thickened, 15 to 20 minutes. Season with salt and pepper. Let cool at room temperature. May be refrigerated, covered, up to 3 days; use at room temperature. Makes 2 to 2½ cups.

FOR THE CHICKEN:

4 whole chickens (about 2½ pounds each), butterflied (see Note).
¼ cup olive oil
Kosher salt and freshly ground pepper
Sherry Vinegar–Brown Sugar Barbecue Baste

Preheat a gas or charcoal grill to medium.

Brush chickens on both sides with olive oil and season with salt and pepper. Grill skin-side down without turning until the skin is golden brown and crispy, 4 to 5 minutes. Turn, and continue grilling until cooked through, 15 to 20 minutes, turning occasionally. Baste with the barbecue baste every 3 minutes.

Place the chickens on a large platter and cut in half.

NOTE: To butterfly a chicken, split it down the backbone and open it out flat.

GRILLED CHICKEN COBB SALAD WITH SMOKED CHILE–BUTTERMILK DRESSING

MAKES 8 SERVINGS

This updated version of California's famous salad makes one of Mesa Grill's most popular lunch dishes. Chicken breast rubbed with barbecue sauce and grilled is a terrific foundation for all the different flavors that combine in a Cobb salad, and chiles jump-start the creamy, tart dressing.

FOR THE BALSAMIC-MUSTARD VINAIGRETTE:

6 tablespoons balsamic vinegar

1 teaspoon Dijon mustard

2 tablespoons finely chopped red onion

1 tablespoon light brown sugar

¾ cup olive oil

Kosher salt and freshly ground pepper

Combine the vinegar, mustard, onion, and sugar in a blender and puree. With the motor running, slowly add the oil until emulsified. Season with salt and pepper. May be refrigerated for 1 day; serve at room temperature. Makes about 1½ cups.

FOR THE SMOKED CHILE–BUTTERMILK DRESSING:

¼ cup sour cream

1 cup buttermilk

2 cloves garlic, finely chopped

2 tablespoons finely chopped red onion

1 tablespoon fresh lime juice

2 teaspoons chipotle puree (see Note)

Kosher salt and freshly ground pepper

Combine the sour cream, buttermilk, garlic, onion, lime juice, and chipotle puree in a small bowl and season with salt and pepper. Pour into a squeeze bottle. May be refrigerated for 1 day; serve at room temperature. Makes about 1¼ cups.

FOR THE SALAD:

4 chicken breasts, skin on and bone in,
    French cut (wings left on)

Kosher salt and freshly ground pepper

1½ cups Mesa Barbecue Sauce (page 29)

2 large red onions, sliced ¼ inch thick

Olive oil for brushing the onions

8 cups mixed greens, washed and dried

Balsamic-Mustard Vinaigrette

8 plum tomatoes, quartered

8 hard-boiled eggs, quartered

4 avocados, peeled, halved, and thinly sliced

8 ounces Cabrales blue cheese, crumbled

Smoked Chile–Buttermilk Dressing

(continued)

45

Preheat a gas or charcoal grill to medium high.

Season the chicken on both sides with salt and pepper and brush with barbecue sauce. Grill, basting continuously with barbecue sauce, until golden brown and cooked through, 7 to 8 minutes on each side. Remove from the grill and let rest for 10 minutes.

Brush the onion slices with olive oil and grill until golden brown and slightly softened, 2 to 3 minutes on each side.

In a large bowl, lightly toss the greens with the Balsamic-Mustard Vinaigrette and place on a large platter. Cut the chicken breasts in half and cut each half on the bias into ½-inch slices. Arrange the chicken in the center of the platter, resting on the greens. Arrange the tomatoes, eggs, onion slices, and avocado slices around the chicken. Sprinkle with the crumbled Cabrales blue cheese and drizzle with the Smoked Chile–Buttermilk Dressing.

NOTE: Canned chipotle peppers in adobo are available at Hispanic or gourmet markets or from Kitchen Market, 218 Eighth Avenue, New York, NY 10011, 212-243-4433, which has a mail-order list.

To make chipotle puree, process canned chipotles in a blender or food processor, along with a little of their liquid.

Red Chile–Citrus Marinated Chicken Breasts with Grilled Tortillas and Avocado-Tomatillo Salsa

MAKES 8 SERVINGS

Try this upscale version of fajitas made on your grill. With grilled chicken breast, grilled tortillas, and a piquant Avocado-Tomatillo Salsa, your guests can build their own spicy creations. (Tomatillos, which look like baby green tomatoes wrapped in papery husks, have a tart, citrusy flavor. They aren't tomatoes at all, but are in the gooseberry family.)

FOR THE RED CHILE–CITRUS MARINADE:

    1 cup fresh orange juice
    1 cup fresh lime juice
    ½ cup fresh lemon juice
    ¼ cup ancho chile powder (see Note 1)
    2 tablespoons paprika
    4 cloves garlic, peeled and coarsely chopped
    1 cup olive oil

Whisk together the juices, chile powder, paprika, garlic, and olive oil in a large bowl until combined. Reserve 1 cup of the marinade. May be refrigerated for 1 day; use at room temperature. Makes about 4 cups.

(continued)

FOR THE AVOCADO-TOMATILLO SALSA:

3 large, ripe Haas avocados, peeled and coarsely chopped

½ cup finely chopped red onion

3 tomatillos, husked, washed, and coarsely chopped

1 jalapeño pepper, finely chopped

3 tablespoons fresh lime juice

3 tablespoons finely chopped cilantro

Kosher salt and freshly ground pepper

Combine the avocados, onion, tomatillos, jalapeño, lime juice, and cilantro in a medium bowl and season with salt and pepper. May be refrigerated, covered, for 1 day; serve at room temperature. Makes 2 cups.

FOR THE CHICKEN BREASTS:

8 chicken breasts, skin on and bone in

Kosher salt and freshly ground pepper

Place the chicken breasts in a large shallow pan or baking dish, add 3 cups of the marinade, and turn to coat completely. Refrigerate, covered, 1 hour or up to 4 hours, turning once.

Preheat a gas or charcoal grill to medium high.

Remove the chicken from the marinade, shaking off any excess, and season on both sides with salt and pepper. (Discard the used marinade.)

Grill the breasts, skin-side down, until golden brown, about 4 minutes. Turn them over, baste with some of the reserved marinade, and cook 4 additional minutes. Repeat turning and basting twice more for a total cooking time of 16 minutes, or until the chicken is well browned and cooked through. Remove the chicken to a platter, cover, and let sit for 10 minutes.

48

FOR THE GRILLED TORTILLAS:

Olive oil for brushing the tortillas

Sixteen 6-inch flour tortillas (or cut 8-inch tortillas to size using a 6-inch plate as a guide)

Kosher salt and freshly ground pepper

Brush each tortilla on both sides with olive oil and season with salt and pepper. Grill along with the chicken until softened, 1 minute on each side.

TO SERVE:

Grilled Chicken Breasts

3 poblano peppers, grilled and julienned (see Note 2)

Avocado-Tomatillo Salsa

Grilled Tortillas

Place the chicken on a large platter and surround with the julienned poblanos. Serve the grilled tortillas and Avocado-Tomatillo Salsa on the side.

NOTES:

1. Ancho chile powder is available at Hispanic or gourmet markets, or from Kitchen Market, 218 Eighth Avenue, New York, NY 10011, 212-243-4433, which has a mail-order list.

2. To grill poblanos, brush with olive oil and season with salt and pepper. Grill over high heat until charred on all sides. Place in a bowl, cover with plastic wrap, and let sit for 15 minutes. Then peel, halve, and seed.

49

Red-Hot Marinated Chicken Skewers with Yogurt-Cilantro Sauce

MAKES 8 SERVINGS

When I was in Greece, I discovered skewered chicken served with yogurt-based sauces. What a great combination! The very simple yogurt sauce I put together cools the spicy heat of the marinade and mellows out the dish, as the Greek sauces do.

FOR THE RED-HOT MARINADE:

1 teaspoon chile de arbol powder (see Note 1)

1 teaspoon cascabel chile powder (see Note 1)

1 tablespoon ancho chile powder (see Note 1)

1 teaspoon cayenne

1 tablespoon cumin seeds, ground (measure before grinding)

1 tablespoon honey

1 cup olive oil

2 cups fresh orange juice

Combine all the ingredients in a large bowl.

FOR THE YOGURT-CILANTRO SAUCE:

1 cup plain low-fat yogurt, drained (see Note 2)

2 tablespoons finely chopped cilantro

2 cloves garlic, minced

1 tablespoon lime juice

Kosher salt and freshly ground pepper

Combine all the ingredients in a medium bowl and season with salt and pepper. Let sit at room temperature for 30 minutes before serving, to blend the flavors. May be refrigerated for 1 day; serve at room temperature. Makes about 1 cup.

FOR THE CHICKEN:

Red-Hot Marinade
8 skinless and boneless chicken thighs, halved lengthwise
32 wooden skewers
Kosher salt
Sixteen 8-inch flour tortillas

Place the chicken in a large baking dish, add the marinade, and turn to coat. Refrigerate, covered, 4 to 6 hours or overnight.

Soak the wooden skewers in water for 2 hours. Preheat a gas or charcoal grill to high.

Remove the chicken from the marinade, shaking off any excess (discard the used marinade).

Thread one skewer through the right side of each chicken thigh and one through the left, so that the meat will stay flat on the grill, and season with salt. Grill until cooked through, about 4 minutes on each side.

Grill the tortillas just until warmed through, about 1 minute on each side.

Arrange the chicken on a serving platter and drizzle with the Yogurt-Cilantro Sauce. Fold the tortillas in half and place beside the chicken.

NOTES:

1. Chile de arbol, cascabel chile, and ancho chile powders are available at Hispanic or gourmet markets, or from Kitchen Market, 218 Eighth Avenue, New York, NY 10011, 212-243-4433, which has a mail-order list.

2. To drain yogurt, place it in a cheesecloth-lined strainer over a bowl for 1 hour, until thickened. Discard the liquid that remains in the bowl.

51

Barbecued Chicken Quesadillas with Grilled Tomato Salsa and Buttermilk Dressing

MAKES 8 SERVINGS

Quesadillas are an excellent way to use leftover chicken. If you make extra grilled chicken for dinner, the next day you are all set for lunch—and that's your weekend. But these are so good, they're worth making from scratch.

In the Grilled Tomato Salsa, the tomatoes are chopped coarsely and are barely cooked, because you want them to retain their shape, texture, and freshness.

FOR THE BUTTERMILK DRESSING:

¼ cup sour cream

1 cup buttermilk

2 cloves garlic, finely chopped

2 tablespoons finely chopped red onion

2 tablespoons fresh lime juice

1 teaspoon cayenne

Kosher salt and freshly ground pepper

In a small bowl, combine sour cream, buttermilk, garlic, onion, lime juice, and cayenne and mix well. Season with salt and pepper. May be refrigerated, covered, for 1 day; serve at room temperature. Makes about 1½ cups.

FOR THE GRILLED TOMATO SALSA:

10 ripe plum tomatoes

2 tablespoons olive oil

Kosher salt and freshly ground pepper

1 jalapeño pepper, finely chopped

4 cloves garlic, finely chopped

2 tablespoons balsamic vinegar

¼ cup coarsely chopped cilantro

Preheat a gas or charcoal grill to low to medium.

Toss the tomatoes with 1 tablespoon of the olive oil and season with salt and pepper. Grill just until the skins are blackened, remove from the grill, and chop coarsely.

In a small bowl, mix the tomatoes with the remaining tablespoon of olive oil, the jalapeño, garlic, vinegar, and cilantro. Season with salt and pepper. May be refrigerated for 1 day; serve at room temperature. Makes about 4 cups.

FOR THE QUESADILLAS:

4 chicken thighs (about 1 pound), boned and skinned

3 cups Mesa Barbecue Sauce (page 29)

Kosher salt and freshly ground pepper

Twenty-four 6-inch flour tortillas (or cut 8-inch tortillas to size, using a 6-inch plate as a guide)

2 cups shredded Monterey Jack cheese

2 cups shredded white Cheddar cheese

1 large red onion, thinly sliced

¼ cup olive oil

2 tablespoons ancho chile powder (see Note)

Grilled Tomato Salsa

Buttermilk Dressing

(continued)

Place the chicken thighs in a shallow pan or baking dish and pour 2 cups of Mesa Barbecue Sauce over them. Refrigerate, covered, for 2 to 4 hours.

Preheat a gas or charcoal grill to high.

Remove the chicken from the marinade, shaking off any excess (discard the used marinade). Season with salt and pepper and grill until cooked through, 6 to 7 minutes on each side. Transfer to a plate and let cool. When cool enough to handle, remove the chicken from the bone and shred. Toss with the remaining cup of barbecue sauce.

Place 8 tortillas on a work surface and top each with 2 tablespoons of each cheese, a slice or two of onion, and some chicken. Cover with another tortilla layer and repeat. Top with a final layer of tortillas, brush with oil, and sprinkle with the chile powder. Grill oiled-side down until golden brown, 3 to 4 minutes.

Place on a serving platter and cut into quarters. Top each quarter with a dollop of Grilled Tomato Salsa and drizzle with the Buttermilk Dressing.

NOTE: Ancho chile powder is available at Hispanic or gourmet markets, or from Kitchen Market, 218 Eighth Avenue, New York, NY 10011, 212-243-4433, which has a mail-order list.

LARRY'S TANGERINE-GLAZED CHICKEN SKEWERS

MAKES 8 SERVINGS

Larry Manheim, one of my talented chefs, makes it into every book I write. This recipe started with one of my ideas that Larry refined. He took a dish that I did and simply added tangerine juice to it, and it's totally delicious. (If you don't have tangerine juice, you can use orange.) Glaze the chicken skewers when they're almost done, just as they're coming off the grill.

FOR THE TANGERINE GLAZE:

¼ cup olive oil

2 shallots, finely diced

½ teaspoon cascabel chile powder (see Note)

1 cup red wine vinegar

1 cup red wine

2 cups tangerine juice

2 tablespoons sugar

Fresh lemon juice to taste

Honey to taste

Kosher salt and freshly ground pepper

Heat 2 tablespoons of the olive oil until almost smoking in a medium saucepan over medium heat. Add the shallots and cascabel powder and cook until the shallots are soft, 3 to 4 minutes. Raise the heat to high, add the vinegar, wine, tangerine juice, and sugar, and cook until reduced to a syrup. Strain into a small mixing bowl and season with lemon juice and honey to taste. Add the remaining 2 tablespoons of olive oil and season with salt and pepper. Let cool at room temperature. May be refrigerated for 1 day; use at room temperature. Makes about 2 cups.

(continued)

FOR THE CITRUS MARINADE:

½ cup fresh orange juice

½ cup fresh lime juice

¼ cup fresh lemon juice

2 tablespoons ancho chile powder (see Note)

1 tablespoon pasilla chile powder (see Note)

2 tablespoons paprika

½ teaspoon cayenne

¼ cup olive oil

Combine all the ingredients in a medium bowl. May be refrigerated for 1 day; use at room temperature. Makes about 1½ cups.

FOR THE CHICKEN:

8 boneless, skinless chicken thighs, halved lengthwise

Citrus Marinade

32 bamboo skewers, soaked in water for 2 hours

Kosher salt

Tangerine Glaze

Place the chicken thighs in a shallow baking pan or baking dish and cover with the marinade. Refrigerate, covered, 2 hours, no longer.

Preheat a gas or charcoal grill to high.

Remove the chicken from the marinade, shaking off any excess (discard the used marinade). Thread one skewer through the right side of each chicken thigh and one through the left, so that the meat will stay flat on the grill, and season with salt. Grill until cooked through, about 4 minutes on each side. Remove the chicken from the grill and brush liberally with the Tangerine Glaze.

Place the chicken skewers on a large serving platter.

NOTE: Cascabel, ancho, and pasilla chile powders are available at Hispanic or gourmet markets, or from Kitchen Market, 218 Eighth Avenue, New York, NY 10011, 212-243-4433, which has a mail-order list.

Indonesian-Style Chicken with Green Onion–Yogurt Sauce

MAKES 8 SERVINGS

Here is a good example of the smooth tanginess of yogurt played off against the spiciness of a marinade. Crunchy green onions (also called scallions), the best the farmers' market has to offer, provide a textural contrast to the sauce.

FOR THE GREEN ONION–YOGURT SAUCE:

2 cups plain yogurt, drained (see Note 1)

½ cup finely sliced green onions, white bulb and 3 inches of the green stem

2 tablespoons fresh lime juice

2 cloves garlic, finely chopped

1 teaspoon honey

1 teaspoon ancho chile powder (see Note 2)

Kosher salt and freshly ground pepper

Combine the yogurt, green onions, lime juice, garlic, honey, chile powder, salt, and pepper in a small mixing bowl and refrigerate, covered, for 2 hours or up to 1 day. Serve at room temperature. Makes about 2½ cups.

(continued)

57

FOR THE INDONESIAN MARINADE:

1 cup olive oil

1 cup fresh lime juice (12 to 16 medium limes)

½ cup fresh lemon juice (2 to 4 medium lemons)

3 tablespoons peeled and minced gingerroot

6 cloves garlic, coarsely chopped

2 tablespoons soy sauce

2 serrano peppers, coarsely chopped

¼ cup coarsely chopped cilantro

4 dashes habañero chile sauce (see Note 2)

2 tablespoons honey

Combine all the ingredients in a mixing bowl and whisk until smooth.

FOR THE CHICKEN:

4 chickens, about 2½ pounds each, quartered

Indonesian Marinade

Kosher salt and freshly ground pepper

Place the chicken in a large, shallow pan or baking dish, cover with the marinade, and turn to coat completely. Refrigerate, covered, up to 2 hours.

Preheat a gas or charcoal grill to high.

Remove the chicken from the marinade and shake off any excess. (Discard the used marinade.) Season with salt and pepper. Grill skin-side down until golden brown, 5 to 6 minutes. Turn and grill flesh-side down until cooked through, 10 to 12 minutes.

Arrange the chicken on a serving platter and serve the yogurt sauce on the side.

NOTES:

1. To drain yogurt, place it in a cheesecloth-lined strainer over a bowl for 1 hour, until thickened. Discard the liquid that remains in the bowl.

2. Ancho chile powder and habañero chile sauce are available at Hispanic or gourmet markets, or from Kitchen Market, 218 Eighth Avenue, New York, NY 10011, 212-243-4433, which has a mail-order list.

Jerked Chicken with Mango-Cilantro Relish and Barbecued Red Onions

MAKES 8 SERVINGS

Spicy Jamaican marinade adds lots of fire to the chicken, but the hot peppers are balanced by the ripe fruit and the brown sugar. If you like, you can substitute pineapple, papaya, or any juicy fruit for the mango in Mango-Cilantro Relish, as long as you keep the contrast going between the savoriness of the chicken and the sweetness of the fruit.

FOR THE MANGO-CILANTRO RELISH:

2 ripe mangoes, peeled and diced
½ red onion, finely sliced
2 tablespoons finely chopped cilantro
2 tablespoons fresh lime juice
2 tablespoons fresh orange juice
2 tablespoons olive oil
Kosher salt and freshly ground pepper

Combine the mangoes, onion, cilantro, citrus juices, and olive oil in a medium bowl and season with salt and pepper. Let sit 30 minutes at room temperature. May be refrigerated for 1 day; serve at room temperature. Makes 4 cups.

(continued)

FOR THE JERK MARINADE:

2 cups vegetable oil

2 large yellow onions, coarsely chopped

4 scallions, coarsely chopped

3 scotch bonnet or habañero peppers, stemmed and seeded

3 tablespoons peeled and grated fresh gingerroot

6 cloves garlic, coarsely chopped

2 tablespoons finely chopped fresh thyme

½ cup red wine vinegar

3 tablespoons light brown sugar

¼ teaspoon cinnamon

¼ teaspoon freshly ground nutmeg

Pinch ground cloves

2 teaspoons ground allspice

2 tablespoons fresh lime juice

Process all the ingredients in a food processor until smooth. May be refrigerated, covered, for 1 day. Makes about 3 cups.

FOR THE CHICKEN:

8 chicken thighs

8 chicken legs

Kosher salt and freshly ground pepper

Pierce the chicken with a fork all over. Place it in a large shallow pan or baking dish. Cover with the marinade and rub it in well. Refrigerate, covered, for 24 or up to 48 hours, depending upon how intense you want the flavor to be.

Preheat a gas or charcoal grill to medium.

Remove the chicken from the marinade, shaking off the excess (discard the used marinade). Season with salt and pepper and grill the chicken until golden brown and cooked through, 5 to 6 minutes on each side.

**16 slices of red onions, ½ inch thick
(don't let the slices separate into rings)**
Mesa Barbecue Sauce (page 29) for brushing
Kosher salt and freshly ground pepper

Brush the onions on both sides with the sauce and season with salt and pepper.

On the preheated gas or charcoal grill, cook slightly, just to obtain grill marks, about 3 minutes on each side.

Arrange the chicken and red onions on a large platter and serve the Mango-Cilantro Relish alongside.

61

Duck Breasts with Fresh Plum-Ginger Glaze and Tomatillo Relish

MAKES 8 SERVINGS

I like grilling duck breast, but you have to be careful and cook it slowly, at low on your gas grill or on a cool part of your charcoal grill. You want the skin to get crispy and the meat to be very tender. For the Plum-Ginger Glaze, get the freshest plums you can find at the farmers' market. With the tomatillos adding tartness to the plums and ginger, you get three different flavors working at once.

FOR THE SPICY PLUM-GINGER SAUCE:

¼ cup peanut oil

2 shallots, finely chopped

4 cloves garlic, finely chopped

2 Thai chiles (available at Asian markets), seeded and finely chopped

2 tablespoons peeled and finely chopped fresh gingerroot

1 tablespoon good quality curry powder

½ teaspoon ground cinnamon

1 star anise, or 1 teaspoon Chinese five-spice powder (both available at Asian markets and some supermarkets)

8 purple plums, pitted and coarsely chopped

¼ cup honey

2 tablespoons soy sauce

¼ cup fresh lime juice

2 tablespoons brown sugar

Preheat a gas or charcoal grill to medium, or use a side burner (or the stove).

Heat the oil until almost smoking in a large nonreactive saucepan and cook the shallots and garlic until soft. Add the Thai chiles, gingerroot, curry powder, and cinnamon, and cook for 2 minutes. Add the remaining ingredients and cook until the sauce becomes thick and has reduced to 4 cups, 30 to 40 minutes. Remove from the heat and let cool slightly at room temperature.

Place the plum mixture, in batches, in a food processor and process until smooth. Strain into a large bowl and let cool completely at room temperature. May be refrigerated for 1 day; serve at room temperature. Makes about 4 cups.

FOR THE TOMATILLO RELISH:

10 tomatillos, husked, washed, and coarsely chopped
¼ cup finely chopped red onion
2 cloves garlic, finely chopped
1 serrano pepper, finely chopped
3 tablespoons fresh lime juice
3 tablespoons coarsely chopped cilantro
1 tablespoon olive oil
1 teaspoon honey
Kosher salt and freshly ground pepper

Combine the tomatillos, onion, garlic, serrano pepper, lime juice, cilantro, olive oil, and honey in a medium bowl and season with salt and pepper. May be refrigerated, covered, for 1 day; serve at room temperature. Makes about 3 cups.

(continued)

CHICKEN AND OTHER POULTRY

FOR THE DUCK:

2 whole boned Muscovy duck breasts with skin left on (about 2 pounds each)
Kosher salt and freshly ground pepper
4 cups Plum-Ginger Sauce
Tomatillo Relish

Preheat a gas or charcoal grill to medium low.

Season the breasts with salt and pepper on both sides and grill, skin-side down, for 5 minutes. Baste, using 3 cups of the plum sauce, turn, baste again, and grill for 5 minutes. Baste, turn, and baste again; cover the grill and cook, skin-side down, for another 5 minutes. Baste, turn, and baste again; cover and cook another 5 minutes, or until well browned on the outside but medium rare on the inside. Total grilling time will be about 20 minutes.

Place the duck breasts on a platter and brush with the remaining cup of plum sauce. Cover with foil and let sit 10 minutes. Cut the breasts on the bias into 1-inch-thick slices. Serve with Tomatillo Relish alongside.

Spit-Roasted Duck Lacquered with Spicy Orange Glaze

MAKES 8 SERVINGS

This impressive looking and tasting duck will remind you of the beautiful specimens displayed in authentic Chinese shops. You will need to cook it on a rotisserie—it will burn if grilled over direct heat. An indoor electric rotisserie, which usually isn't effective for dishes that require really high heat, will do a good job here.

FOR THE GLAZE:

- 2 tablespoons olive oil
- 1 red onion, coarsely chopped
- 4 cloves garlic, coarsely chopped
- 6 cups fresh orange juice
- 2 tablespoons soy sauce
- 1 star anise (available at Asian markets and some supermarkets)
- 2 tablespoons red chile paste (available at Asian markets and some supermarkets)

Heat the olive oil until almost smoking in a medium saucepan over medium-high heat, and cook the onion and garlic until soft. Add the orange juice, soy sauce, anise, and chile paste and bring to a boil. Cook until reduced to 3 cups. Transfer the mixture to a blender and blend until smooth. Let cool to room temperature. May be refrigerated for 1 day; use at room temperature. Makes about 3 cups.

(continued)

FOR THE DUCKS:

2 whole ducks (4½ pounds each)
Kosher salt and freshly ground pepper

Place the ducks in a large, shallow pan or baking dish and cover with 2 cups of the marinade. Refrigerate, covered, 4 to 6 hours or overnight.

Preheat a gas or charcoal grill to low. Remove the ducks from the marinade and shake off any excess (discard the used marinade). Place the ducks on a spit and grill over low heat until done, about 2 hours, basting occasionally with the reserved cup of marinade.

Carve the ducks into quarters and place on a serving platter.

Jack's Turkey Porterhouse Steaks

MAKES 8 SERVINGS

Jack McDavid, my TV partner on *Grillin' and Chillin'*, is an innovative chef who came up with a new take on turkey breast. Cut the whole breast down the middle, against the grain, to get a piece of meat that resembles a porterhouse steak. Each piece will have a bone in the center and will grill beautifully.

FOR THE DRY RUB:

1¼ cups Hungarian paprika
1 tablespoon celery salt
2 teaspoons dried sage
1 tablespoon dry mustard
1 tablespoon ancho chile powder (see Note)

Combine all the ingredients in a small bowl.

FOR THE TURKEY:

8 slices turkey porterhouse, ¾ inch thick
¼ cup peanut oil

Place the turkey steaks in a large shallow pan or baking dish. Rub on both sides with the dry rub and let sit at room temperature for 1 hour.

Preheat a gas or charcoal grill to medium high.

Brush the steaks with peanut oil and grill until golden brown, 4 to 5 minutes. Turn and grill on the other side until cooked through, 5 to 6 minutes.

NOTE: Ancho chile powder is available at Hispanic or gourmet markets, or mail order from Kitchen Market, 218 Eighth Avenue, New York, NY 10011, 212-243-4433.

67

Turkey Breast Marinated in Molasses, Orange, Ginger, and Garlic with Orange-Pomegranate Relish

MAKES 8 SERVINGS

This is a far cry from your Thanksgiving turkey (although the relish gives a nod to tradition), and it's a good way to pump lots of strong flavors into that normally bland fowl. Give the turkey a long enough time to marinate, then grill it quickly. Wrapping it in foil after the initial searing protects it from losing all those delicious juices.

FOR THE MOLASSES-ORANGE MARINADE:

2½ cups freshly squeezed orange juice

1 cup light molasses

2 tablespoons peeled and coarsely chopped fresh gingerroot

6 cloves garlic, coarsely chopped

4 fresh sage leaves, chiffonade (see Note)

Combine all the ingredients in a medium bowl. May be refrigerated for 1 day; use at room temperature. Makes 3 cups.

FOR THE ORANGE-POMEGRANATE RELISH:

3 oranges, peeled and sectioned

½ cup pomegranate seeds (cut a pomegranate in half and spoon out the seeds)

¼ cup finely chopped red onion

½ small bulb of fennel, cut into julienne
(small matchstick-size pieces)

¼ cup fresh orange juice

2 tablespoons fresh lime juice

2 tablespoons olive oil

1 tablespoon honey

Kosher salt and freshly ground pepper

2 tablespoons chervil leaves

Combine the orange sections, pomegranate seeds, onion, fennel, orange juice, lime juice, olive oil, and honey in a medium bowl and season with salt and pepper. Let sit at room temperature 30 minutes. Add the chervil after the 30-minute rest. May be refrigerated for 1 day without the chervil; add it just before serving. Serve at room temperature. Makes 1½ to 2 cups.

FOR THE TURKEY BREAST:

One 4-pound boneless turkey breast

3 cups Molasses-Orange Marinade

Kosher salt and freshly ground pepper

Place the turkey in a large shallow pan or baking dish, pour 2 cups of the marinade over it, and turn to coat. Refrigerate, covered, 2 to 4 hours or overnight.

Preheat a gas or charcoal grill to medium high. Remove the turkey from the marinade, shaking off the excess (discard the used marinade), and season with salt and pepper. Grill skin-side down until crisp, 5 to 6 minutes. Baste with some of the reserved marinade, turn over, and baste again. Reduce the heat to medium, wrap the turkey in aluminum foil, and continue cooking until a meat thermometer registers 165°F, about 20 minutes. Remove from the grill and let rest 10 minutes.

Slice the turkey on the bias ½ inch thick and arrange on a serving platter. Top with spoonfuls of the Orange-Pomegranate Relish.

NOTE: To cut sage into chiffonade, or fine ribbons, roll up the leaves and cut into thin strips.

69

CHICKEN AND OTHER POULTRY

4. FINS AND SHELLS

Fish and shellfish on the grill are becoming more and more mainstream. They may not be the first thing you think of when you plan to barbecue, but their popularity is growing fast. Many people, including me, consider grilling to be the best possible way to cook fish (stovetop searing combined with finishing in the oven is second). It cooks them through quickly, searing the outside and keeping the center juicy and tender.

It's important to work with the right kind of fish, especially if you are a newcomer to grilling. Buy the best and freshest, checking that it is sweet-smelling and firm to the touch. Go for meaty, thick steak fish, such as tuna, shark, or salmon, rather than thin fillets, such as flounder or sole. A one-inch-thick fish steak will stay together on the grill and won't give you any problems when you want to turn it; this isn't true for a delicate fillet. But red snapper fillets cook beautifully wrapped in corn husks, as do salmon fillets grilled on heated cedar "planks," Native American style.

On the barbecue, the simplest treatment is the best, and it's fine just to brush fish steaks with olive oil, season with salt and pepper, and grill quickly over high heat. An herbal crust or a fruity glaze adds a little more sophistication to tuna steaks, or brush them with balsamic vinegar as they cook. Some cooks marinate fish for a little while, but I'd much rather put a relish or a sauce on it later. It's cleaner—if you buy a really good piece of fish, you don't want to interrupt the flavor.

Whole fish, usually one per person, also benefit from simple cooking and pairing later with sharp Horseradish-Tomato Vinaigrette, Lemon-Tarragon Oil, or Warm Asian Vinaigrette.

Shrimp on the grill are so quick and easy, I like to throw them on when my guests arrive and serve them as walking-around food before I start the main course. Thread them onto skewers so they stay together, cook easily, and come off the grate with no trouble. You can marinate shrimp because they are more dense than fish steaks or fillets, but keep it short, or the marinade will start to "cook" them. This enzymatic cooking is what happens to scallops in Ceviche, and I give the process a little nudge by searing the scallops first, for extra flavor and texture. Also try scallops enhanced with pineapple two ways: first in a spicy glaze while they cook briefly, then with Grilled Pineapple Relish served alongside.

Softshell crab is a great springtime and summer treat, and I love to serve it to my guests. You can cook it either directly on the grill or in a heated pan set on the grate. Serve the crisp grilled crab in sandwiches, dressed with basil pesto, and the sautéed crab in a hot chile and lemon-brown butter that you make in the pan.

A large, heavy saucepan also allows you to steam clams or mussels right on the grill. Cover the pan and let them steam on one side of the fire while you grill corn or eggplant on the other.

The grill is a natural for Paella, a dish of several components that are cooked separately and combined shortly before serving. It's a cinch to grill each part in sequence, keeping your fire going and your guests involved in the process.

Lobster is awesome on the barbecue, but take care that it doesn't dry out or burn. The best way to avoid this is to steam or boil the lobster first, then split it and grill just long enough to impart a subtle smoky flavor and a slight char. When it comes off the fire, drown it with lush herbal butter. For lobster feasts, I recommend that your guests protect their clothes with large bibs or aprons, or easier still, wear bathing suits.

RECIPES

Herb-Crusted Tuna with Lemony
  Cracked Wheat Salad

Mango-Glazed Tuna Steaks
  with Black Bean Salad

Tuna Steaks Brushed with Fresh Mint,
  with Fig and Nectarine Relish

Grilled Tuna Salad Sandwiches with
  Whole Grain Mustard Mayonnaise
  on Grilled Rye Bread

Whole Brook Trout with
  Lemon-Tarragon Oil

Whole Brook Trout with Fresh
  Horseradish-Tomato Vinaigrette

Lemon-Glazed Whole Red Snapper
  with Fresh Herbes de Provence

Whole Red Snapper with Warm Asian
  Vinaigrette

Red Snapper Grilled in Corn Husks
  with Roasted Jalapeño–Lime Butter

Cedar Plank–Grilled Salmon
  with Yellow Pepper–Saffron Sauce

Red Chile–Rubbed Salmon with
  Toasted Corn Vinaigrette

Striped Bass with Red Wine–Shallot
  Butter and Grilled Green Onions

Garlic Shrimp Splashed with
  Sherry Vinegar

Ginger-Marinated Shrimp with
  Toasted Sesame Seed Vinaigrette

Barbecue Sauce–Soaked Shrimp
  with Crème Fraîche Dressing

Grilled Shrimp Cocktail with
  Tomato-Horseradish Dipping Sauce

Spicy Shrimp with Asian
  Peanut Dipping Sauce

Shrimp Skewered on Rosemary Branches

Smoked Chile Butter–Brushed Shrimp
  with Tomatillo Salsa

Spicy Pineapple-Glazed Sea Scallops
  with Soy-Miso Vinaigrette
  and Grilled Pineapple Relish

Grilled Sea Scallop Ceviche

Softshell Crab Sandwiches with Basil
  Pesto Dressing and Jicama Slaw

Sautéed Softshell Crabs with
  Lemon-Brown Butter and
  Scotch Bonnet Chile

Whole Lobster Smothered in
  Cascabel Chile Butter

Lobster Tails with Curry-Mango Butter

Lobster Rolls with Curried Mayonnaise

Grilled Lobster Quesadillas with
  Yellow Tomato–Roasted Garlic Salsa

Paella on the Grill

Steamed Littleneck Clams with Chorizo
  and Fresh Corn

Littleneck Clams Steamed in
  Green Chile–Coconut Milk Broth

Squid with Avocado-Tomato Salad
  and Smoked Chile Dressing

Squid with Grilled Tomato–Bread Salad

Grilled Squid Salad with Papaya,
  Green Onions, and Peanuts

73

FINS AND SHELLS

Herb-Crusted Tuna with Lemony Cracked Wheat Salad

MAKES 8 SERVINGS

This combination is one of Bolo's most popular summertime dishes. The light, citrus-flavored cracked wheat salad makes the perfect backdrop for the fresh herbs, lemon zest, and garlic that crust the grilled tuna.

FOR THE LEMONY CRACKED WHEAT SALAD:

3 cups bulgur wheat

1 medium red onion, finely chopped

2 large tomatoes, seeded and finely diced

2 cloves garlic, finely chopped

¼ cup coarsely chopped cilantro

½ cup coarsely chopped parsley

¼ cup fresh lemon juice

1 tablespoon finely grated lemon zest

2 tablespoons honey

¼ cup olive oil

Kosher salt and freshly ground pepper

Place the bulgur in a large bowl and cover with boiling water. Cover the bowl and let sit 15 minutes. Fluff with a fork. Add the onion, tomatoes, garlic, and herbs, and mix. In a small bowl, whisk together the lemon juice, lemon zest, honey, and olive oil and add to the mixture. Stir well and season with salt and pepper.

¾ **cup olive oil**

¼ **cup finely chopped flat-leaf parsley**

¼ **cup finely chopped chervil**

3 **tablespoons finely chopped tarragon**

1 **tablespoon finely chopped lemon zest**

3 **cloves garlic, finely chopped**

8 **tuna steaks (6 ounces each)**

Kosher salt and freshly ground pepper

Preheat a gas or charcoal grill to medium.

Place the oil, herbs, lemon zest, and garlic in a food processor and process into a smooth paste.

Season the tuna steaks on both sides with salt and pepper and rub with the herb mixture on one side. Grill herb-side down until a crust forms, 2 to 3 minutes. Turn over and grill 2 to 3 minutes more for medium rare (or to desired doneness).

Pile the cracked wheat salad on a large platter and top with the tuna steaks.

MANGO-GLAZED TUNA STEAKS WITH BLACK BEAN SALAD

MAKES 8 SERVINGS

I juggled some of my favorite ingredients to create this play on the tuna tostada we did at the inception of Mesa Grill. Instead of serving a black bean-mango salsa like the one that accompanied the original dish, I use the sweet mangoes to glaze the tuna, and I serve it all with a savory black bean salad. What a great way to do a tuna salad!

(continued)

75

MANGO DRESSING:

1 mango, peeled, pitted, and coarsely chopped

3 tablespoons fresh lime juice

2 cloves garlic, finely chopped

2 tablespoons finely chopped red onion

¼ cup coarsely chopped cilantro

¼ teaspoon cumin

¾ cup olive oil

Kosher salt and freshly ground pepper

Place the mango, lime juice, garlic, onion, cilantro, and cumin in a blender and blend until smooth. With the motor running, slowly add the olive oil until emulsified. Season with salt and pepper. May be refrigerated, covered, for 1 day; serve at room temperature. Makes about 1 cup.

BLACK BEAN SALAD:

1 pound dry black beans, cooked according to package
    directions, or 5½ cups canned black beans, rinsed
    and drained

4 cloves garlic, finely chopped

4 scallions, with 3 inches of the green left on,
    thinly sliced on the diagonal

1 ripe mango, peeled, pitted, and finely chopped

2 ripe tomatoes, seeded and finely diced

Mango Dressing

Kosher salt and freshly ground pepper

Combine the beans, garlic, scallions, mango, and tomatoes in a large bowl. Toss with the Mango Dressing and season with salt and pepper. Serve at room temperature.

For the Tuna

MANGO GLAZE:

- 2 tablespoons olive oil
- ½ cup coarsely chopped Spanish onion
- 2 cloves garlic, coarsely chopped
- 1 serrano pepper, coarsely chopped
- 1 tablespoon peeled and coarsely grated gingerroot
- 4 cups mango nectar (available in Hispanic markets and some supermarkets)
- ¼ cup light brown sugar
- 2 tablespoons red wine vinegar
- Kosher salt and freshly ground pepper

Preheat a gas or charcoal grill to medium, or use a side or stove burner.

Heat the olive oil in a medium nonreactive saucepan until almost smoking. Add the onion and garlic and cook until soft. Add the serrano pepper and ginger and cook for 2 minutes. Add the mango nectar and brown sugar, bring to a boil, and cook until reduced to 2 cups. Place the mixture in a food processor with the vinegar and process until smooth. Season with salt and pepper. Let cool at room temperature. May be refrigerated for 1 day; use at room temperature. Makes about 2½ cups.

TUNA:

- 8 tuna steaks (6 ounces each)
- Mango Glaze
- Kosher salt and freshly ground pepper

Preheat a gas or charcoal grill to medium high. Brush the tuna steaks on both sides with 1½ cups of the Mango Glaze and season with salt and pepper. Grill 2 to 3 minutes on each side for medium-rare doneness. Arrange the steaks on a platter and immediately brush with the remaining cup of Mango Glaze. Serve Black Bean Salad alongside.

77

Tuna Steaks Brushed with Fresh Mint, with Fig and Nectarine Relish

MAKES 8 SERVINGS

Don't be surprised to find fresh mint grilled with tuna, and figs and nectarines combined in a relish. That's what summer grilling is all about!

A handful of fresh mint leaves rubbed into its flesh gives the strong, dense tuna a lot of contrasting flavor. There is mint in the Fig and Nectarine Relish, as well, so you get a double dose of this cooling herb. As for the figs and nectarines, why not take the best fruit you can find at the farmers' market and use it in a relish? Highlight the juicy fruit with contrasting flavors and textures, such as balsamic vinegar and crisp red onion.

FOR THE FIG AND NECTARINE RELISH:

    4 ripe figs, cut into ½-inch dice
    3 ripe nectarines, pitted and cut into ½-inch dice
    ¼ cup finely chopped red onion
    2 tablespoons mint, chiffonade (see Note)
    3 tablespoons aged balsamic vinegar
    2 tablespoons olive oil
    Kosher salt and freshly ground pepper

Combine the figs, nectarines, onion, mint, vinegar, and olive oil in a medium bowl and season with salt and pepper. Let sit at room temperature for 30 minutes. May be refrigerated for 1 day; serve at room temperature. Makes 4 cups.

FOR THE TUNA:

8 tuna steaks (6 ounces each)
¼ cup mint leaves
¼ cup olive oil
Kosher salt and freshly ground pepper

Preheat a gas or charcoal grill to high.

Dip the mint leaves into the olive oil and rub them into both sides of the tuna. Season with salt and pepper. Grill 2 to 3 minutes on each side for rare (or to desired doneness).

Place the tuna on a large serving plate and pile the relish alongside or on top of the fish.

NOTE: To cut mint into chiffonade, or fine ribbons, roll up the leaves and cut into thin strips.

GRILLED TUNA SALAD SANDWICHES WITH WHOLE GRAIN MUSTARD MAYONNAISE ON GRILLED RYE BREAD

MAKES 8 SANDWICHES

Fresh tuna salad is nothing like the canned stuff you order for lunch—it is fish, not mush, with a chewy texture and a briny flavor. If you've bought a big piece of tuna to cut into steaks and grill the night before, you can save the ends to cook the next day for tuna salad. Make a mayonnaise with whole grain mustard, to add spiciness, and serve it on grilled rye bread, for delicious toasty flavor.

(continued)

79

6 tuna steaks (6 ounces each)

Olive oil for brushing the tuna

Kosher salt and freshly ground pepper

1 medium red onion, thinly sliced

1 cup finely chopped celery

12 cornichons, coarsely chopped

1 cup good quality mayonnaise

3 tablespoons whole grain mustard

2 tablespoons fresh lemon juice

¼ cup flat-leaf parsley

1 tablespoon finely chopped thyme leaves

16 slices rye bread (½ inch thick)

Lettuce leaves, for garnish

Tomato slices, for garnish

Preheat a gas or charcoal grill to hot.

Brush the tuna with olive oil and season with salt and pepper on both sides. Grill until cooked medium well, about 4 minutes on each side (or to desired doneness). Remove from the grill and let sit for 10 minutes. Cut the tuna into ¼-inch cubes and place in a large bowl. Add the onion, celery, and cornichons, and mix to combine.

In a small bowl, whisk together the mayonnaise, mustard, and lemon juice and season with salt and pepper. Fold the dressing into the tuna, season with salt and pepper, and add the parsley and thyme.

Grill the bread on both sides until crisp. Divide the tuna salad among 8 slices of bread, garnish with lettuce and tomato, and cover with the remaining bread.

WHOLE BROOK TROUT WITH LEMON-TARRAGON OIL

MAKES 8 SERVINGS

As a kid, I used to go camping in the Adirondacks with my Uncle Tippy, who was a remarkable guy all his life. He had an incredible feel for the wilderness, as if he were part of it. He could tell you if there were deer or bear around, and exactly when and where to go trout fishing. He'd hunt deer in the winter, in all this snow, and that's when I had my first taste of venison—the real, wild stuff.

In the summertime, we would go thirty miles back into the woods to a perfectly clear, untouched stream, get into a canoe, and fish for trout. Then we would cook our catch at night over a fire. It's no wonder that cooking fish outdoors still holds some magic for me.

FOR THE LEMON-TARRAGON OIL:

> 2 cups extra-virgin olive oil
>
> Zest of 2 lemons
>
> ¼ cup tarragon leaves
>
> 1 tablespoon ground toasted fennel seeds

Combine the olive oil, lemon zest, and tarragon in a medium, noncorrosive saucepan and bring to a simmer over medium heat. Remove from the heat, add the fennel seeds, and let steep for 2 hours at room temperature; strain. Can be refrigerated in a tightly covered glass jar up to 2 days; bring to room temperature before serving. Makes 2 cups.

(continued)

FOR THE TROUT:

8 whole trout (1 pound each), cleaned and gutted
Olive oil for brushing the trout
Kosher salt and freshly ground pepper

Preheat a gas or charcoal grill to medium high.

Brush each trout on both sides with olive oil and season with salt and pepper. Grill for 6 to 8 minutes for each ½ inch of thickness, turning fish over halfway through grilling time. Remove the fish from the grill, place on a large serving platter, and drizzle with the Lemon-Tarragon Oil while the fish is still hot.

WHOLE BROOK TROUT WITH FRESH HORSERADISH-TOMATO VINAIGRETTE

MAKES 8 SERVINGS

You can use a blender to make this vinaigrette, unless you're out in the woods, where you can shake up the ingredients in a jar instead.

FOR THE FRESH HORSERADISH-TOMATO VINAIGRETTE:

½ cup red wine vinegar
4 ripe plum tomatoes, seeded: 2 halved and 2 finely diced
2 tablespoons finely grated fresh horseradish, or prepared
    horseradish, drained
½ shallot, coarsely chopped
1 tablespoon honey
¾ cup olive oil
¼ cup flat-leaf parsley
Kosher salt and freshly ground pepper

82

Place the vinegar, halved tomatoes, horseradish, and shallot in a blender and blend until smooth. Add the honey. With the motor running, slowly add the olive oil until emulsified. Remove to a bowl, fold in the finely diced tomatoes and parsley, and season with salt and pepper. May be refrigerated for 1 day; serve at room temperature. Makes about 2 cups.

FOR THE TROUT:

8 whole trout (about 1 pound each), cleaned and scaled
Olive oil for brushing the trout
Kosher salt and freshly ground pepper

Preheat a gas or charcoal grill to high.

Brush each trout on both sides with olive oil and season with salt and pepper. Grill for 6 to 8 minutes for each ½ inch of thickness, turning fish over halfway through grilling time. Place on a large platter and drizzle with Fresh Horseradish-Tomato Vinaigrette. Serve any remaining vinaigrette on the side.

83

FINS AND SHELLS

Lemon-Glazed Whole Red Snapper with Fresh Herbes de Provence

MAKES 8 SERVINGS

We used to roast a glazed whole fish when I worked at Hulot's, a French bistro in New York, and I like to do something similar on the fire. I grill the snapper whole, stuff it with fresh herbs, and glaze it about halfway through. It's very simple and totally delicious.

FOR THE LEMON GLAZE:

¼ cup sugar

½ cup white wine vinegar

2 cups fresh lemon juice

½ cup fresh orange juice

2 shallots, finely chopped

Kosher salt and freshly ground pepper

Preheat a gas or charcoal grill to medium high or use a side burner (or the stove).

In a medium nonreactive saucepan boil the sugar and vinegar until the sugar has dissolved and the mixture has become syrupy, about 5 minutes. Add the lemon and orange juices, and shallots, and simmer until reduced by half. Season with salt and pepper. May be refrigerated up to 2 days; use at room temperature. Makes about 1 cup.

FOR THE SNAPPER:

8 whole red snappers (about 1 pound each), or four 2-pound snappers, scaled and gutted

Olive oil for brushing the fish

Kosher salt and freshly ground pepper

16 sprigs rosemary

24 basil leaves

16 sprigs thyme

24 sprigs parsley

Lemon Glaze

Preheat a gas or charcoal grill to medium high. Brush the fish inside and outside with olive oil and season with salt and pepper. Stuff with herb sprigs and leaves and tie shut with kitchen string (wrap the string around the fish once about one-third of the way down from the head, and once again another third of the way down).

Grill until crisp-skinned and just cooked through, 3 to 4 minutes per side for each ½ inch of thickness, brushing halfway through with the Lemon Glaze. Place on a large serving platter and immediately brush both sides with the remaining glaze.

Whole Red Snapper with Warm Asian Vinaigrette

MAKES 8 SERVINGS

This red snapper is grilled until it's seared on the outside and tender inside, and my version of an Asian vinaigrette gives it exotic flavors.

FOR THE WARM ASIAN VINAIGRETTE:

3 tablespoons olive oil

2 shallot, finely chopped

2 cloves garlic, finely chopped

2 tablespoons peeled and finely grated gingerroot

¼ cup fresh lime juice

1½ cups low-sodium light soy sauce

1 tablespoon honey

1 teaspoon toasted sesame oil

¼ teaspoon freshly ground white pepper

Preheat a gas or charcoal grill to medium high or use a side burner (or a stove).

Heat the oil until almost smoking in a small saucepan. Add the shallots and garlic and cook until soft. Add the gingerroot and continue cooking for 2 minutes. Add the lime juice, soy sauce, honey, and sesame oil and bring to a simmer. Season with white pepper. May be refrigerated for 1 day; serve at room temperature. Makes 2 cups.

FOR THE RED SNAPPER:

**8 whole red snappers (1 pound each),
  or four 2-pound snappers, gutted and scaled**
Olive oil for brushing the snappers
Kosher salt and freshly ground white pepper
Warm Asian Vinaigrette
¼ cup coarsely chopped cilantro

Preheat a gas or charcoal grill to high.

Brush the snappers on both sides with olive oil and season with salt and white pepper. Grill until just cooked through, 3 to 4 minutes per side for each ½ inch of thickness. Transfer to a platter and immediately drizzle with Warm Asian Vinaigrette and chopped cilantro.

87

FINS AND SHELLS

Red Snapper Grilled in Corn Husks with Roasted Jalapeño–Lime Butter

MAKES 8 SERVINGS

This is a favorite at Mesa Grill and it illustrates a good cooking method for fish. The snapper sort of steams in the corn husks and becomes infused with the flavor of corn, but there is more to the dish. As the corn husks char, they transmit their grilled flavor to the fish, as well. Roasted jalapeños back up the grilled note in the compound butter.

FOR THE ROASTED JALAPEÑO–LIME BUTTER

3 jalapeño peppers

Olive oil for rubbing the peppers

1 cup fresh lime juice (12 to 16 medium limes)

1 tablespoon honey

½ teaspoon kosher salt

½ pound (2 sticks) unsalted butter, softened

Preheat a gas or charcoal grill to high.

Rub the peppers with the olive oil and grill, turning, until charred on all sides, 3 to 5 minutes. Peel and seed the peppers and coarsely chop.

In a small saucepan over high heat, bring the lime juice to a boil and reduce to ¼ cup. Place the reduced lime juice, jalapeños, honey, salt, and butter in a food processor and process until smooth.

Place a sheet of parchment or wax paper on a work surface. Form the butter into a roll about 1 inch in diameter and place it along the long side of the paper, leaving a border of 1 inch. Roll up the butter in the paper and refrigerate for 30 minutes or up to 3 days. The butter also may be frozen.

FOR THE RED SNAPPER:

20 corn husks (available at Hispanic markets),
soaked in water for 2 hours
8 red snapper fillets (about 6 ounces each)
Olive oil for brushing the fillets and the corn husk packets
Kosher salt and freshly ground pepper
Roasted Jalapeño–Lime Butter

Preheat a gas or charcoal grill to high.

Brush each fillet with olive oil and season with salt and pepper. Remove the corn husks from the water and pat dry. Cut 2 or 3 corn husks into long, narrow strips. There should be 16 strips.

For each fillet, lay one corn husk flat on a work surface, place the fish inside, and top with a second corn husk. Using the long strips, tie each end, to form a closed packet. Brush the packet with oil and grill 3½ minutes on each side.

To serve, arrange the fish packets on a large platter. Cut open each packet and place a dollop of Roasted Jalapeño–Lime Butter over the fish.

89

Cedar Plank–Grilled Salmon with Yellow Pepper–Saffron Sauce

MAKES 8 SERVINGS

Larry Forgione was the first person I ever saw cooking fish on a cedar plank, or shingle, and since this is a Native American method, it was certainly appropriate for the chef of An American Place.

This is a Mesa Grill–Bolo fusion dish: we cook salmon on a plank at Mesa, and Yellow Pepper–Saffron Sauce is right out of Bolo.

First heat up the planks to release the cedar aroma, then put the fish on top, and, finally, place the whole thing on a grill. Watch very carefully and moderate the heat so the cedar doesn't burn. The salmon cooks slowly in its own fat, so it's moist and delicious.

FOR THE YELLOW PEPPER–SAFFRON SAUCE:

> **2 tablespoons olive oil**
> **1 large onion, coarsely chopped**
> **4 yellow bell peppers, grilled, peeled,
>   and coarsely chopped (see Note)**
> **1 cup white wine**
> **Large pinch of saffron threads**
> **½ cup heavy cream**
> **Kosher salt and freshly ground black pepper**

Heat the olive oil until almost smoking in a medium saucepan over medium-high heat. Add the onion and cook until soft. Add the peppers and continue cooking 10 minutes.

In a small bowl, combine the wine and saffron. Add the wine mixture to the onion mixture, raise the heat to high, and cook until almost dry.

Pour the mixture into a blender and blend until smooth. Return to a clean saucepan over medium heat, add the cream, and simmer 10 minutes. Season with salt and pepper to taste. May be refrigerated for 1 day; serve at room temperature. Makes about 3 cups.

FOR THE SALMON:

Eight 3-by-8-inch untreated cedar shingles (available at lumber yards), soaked in water for 2 hours
Vegetable oil for brushing the cedar shingles
8 salmon fillets (6 ounces each)
Olive oil for brushing the salmon
Kosher salt and freshly ground pepper
Yellow Pepper–Saffron Sauce

Preheat a gas grill to medium, or prepare a charcoal fire.

Remove the shingles from the water and brush with vegetable oil on both sides. Place on the grill and allow to heat through, about 10 minutes. Tear off eight 12-inch squares of aluminum foil and place one shingle on each square, using tongs.

Brush each side of the salmon with olive oil and season with salt and pepper to taste. Place a salmon fillet on each shingle and fold the edges of the foil together on all sides, to seal the pack. Carefully place the packs on the grill and grill until medium well done, 6 to 8 minutes.

Place the salmon packets on a large serving platter and carefully open them. Accompany with a bowl of the Yellow Pepper–Saffron Sauce.

NOTE: To grill the bell peppers, brush with olive oil and season with salt and pepper. Grill over high heat until charred on all sides. Place in a bowl, cover with plastic wrap, and let sit for 15 minutes. Then peel, halve, and seed.

91

FINS AND SHELLS

Red Chile–Rubbed Salmon with Toasted Corn Vinaigrette

MAKES 8 SERVINGS

The sugar in the red chile rub caramelizes the outside of the salmon and provides a crisp crust. Toasted corn vinaigrette brings its own sweet-smoky flavor and gives the dish great freshness.

FOR THE TOASTED CORN VINAIGRETTE:

- **3 ears of corn**
- **¼ cup lime juice**
- **1 jalapeño pepper, grilled and seeded (see Note 1)**
- **½ cup olive oil**
- **2 green onions (white bulb and 3 inches of green), finely sliced**
- **¼ cup coarsely chopped cilantro**
- **Kosher salt and freshly ground pepper**

Preheat a gas or charcoal grill to medium high.

In a large pot of boiling water, blanch the corn about 5 minutes, until not quite cooked through. Place the ears on the grill until slightly charred on all sides, about 2 minutes. Remove from the grill and, with a sharp knife, scrape the kernels into a small bowl. There should be about 1½ cups.

Combine the lime juice and jalapeño in a blender and blend until smooth. With the motor running, slowly add the olive oil until emulsified.

Place the corn and the green onions in a large mixing bowl and pour the pureed mixture over them. Add the cilantro and mix well. Season with salt and pepper. May be refrigerated, covered, for 1 day; serve at room temperature. Makes about 3 cups.

FOR THE RED CHILE SALMON:

8 salmon steaks or fillets (6 ounces each)
½ cup ancho chile powder (see Note 2)
2 teaspoons ground cumin
2 tablespoons brown sugar
1 teaspoon cinnamon
½ cup olive oil
Kosher salt and freshly ground pepper
Toasted Corn Vinaigrette

Preheat a gas or charcoal grill to medium high.

Combine the ancho chile powder, cumin, sugar, cinnamon, and olive oil in a small bowl and season with salt and pepper. Coat the salmon with the mixture on one side only. Grill, pepper-side down, until a crust forms, about 2 minutes. Turn the steaks and cook for 5 more minutes, for medium doneness.

Arrange the salmon on a platter, pepper-side up, and drizzle with the Toasted Corn Vinaigrette. Serve any remaining vinaigrette alongside.

NOTES:

1. To grill the jalapeño, brush with olive oil and season with salt and pepper. Grill over high heat until charred on all sides. Place in a bowl, cover with plastic wrap, and let sit for 15 minutes. Then peel, halve, and seed.

2. Ancho chile powder is available at Hispanic or gourmet markets, or from Kitchen Market, 218 Eighth Avenue, New York, NY 10011, 212-243-4433, which has a mail-order list.

93

Striped Bass with Red Wine–Shallot Butter and Grilled Green Onions

MAKES 8 SERVINGS

Any striped bass you buy will be either wild or farm raised, and they are two different kinds of fish. The wild bass are bigger and meatier and have more flavor; the farm-raised fish are smaller, cleaner tasting, and more consistent in quality.

FOR THE RED WINE–SHALLOT BUTTER:

- 2 tablespoons olive oil
- 1 large shallot, coarsely chopped
- 2 cups dry red wine
- 1 tablespoon coarsely chopped fresh thyme leaves
- ½ pound (2 sticks) unsalted butter, softened
- Kosher salt and freshly ground pepper

On a side burner (or the stove), heat the olive oil over medium heat until almost smoking and cook the shallot until soft, 3 to 4 minutes. Raise the heat to high, add the wine, bring to a boil, and reduce to ¼ cup. Remove from the heat, add the thyme, and let cool to room temperature.

Place the wine mixture in a food processor with the butter and process until smooth. Season with salt and pepper. Place a sheet of parchment or wax paper on a work surface. Form the butter into a roll about 1 inch in diameter and place it along the long side of the paper, leaving a border of 1 inch. Roll up the butter in the paper and refrigerate for 30 minutes or up to 3 days. The butter also may be frozen. Makes about 1½ cups.

FOR THE BASS:

8 whole bass (1 pound each), or four 2-pound bass,
scaled and gutted
Olive oil for brushing the fish
Kosher salt and freshly ground pepper
Red Wine–Shallot Butter

Preheat a gas or charcoal grill to high.

Brush each fish with oil on both sides and season with salt and pepper. Grill until seared on each side, about 2 minutes per side. Then place a piece of aluminum foil under the fish, lower the heat to medium if using a gas grill, or move to a cooler part of the charcoal grill, and continue grilling until cooked through, 4 to 6 minutes.

Place on a serving plate and immediately top with a dollop of Red Wine–Shallot Butter.

FOR THE GREEN ONIONS:

1 bunch green onions, trimmed, all the green left on
Olive oil for brushing
Kosher salt and freshly ground pepper

Brush the green onions with olive oil and season with salt and pepper. Place on the preheated grill and cook until marked and softened, 2 to 3 minutes on each side. Serve with the grilled bass.

95

GARLIC SHRIMP SPLASHED WITH SHERRY VINEGAR

MAKES 8 SERVINGS

Grill the shrimp quickly, as you would scampi, and splash them with vinegar when they are still hot, so they will absorb the tart flavor. This dish takes no time at all and is the perfect appetizer—it opens the palate. Your guests will love munching on the garlicky shrimp while dinner is cooking.

1 cup olive oil

1 head garlic, peeled and coarsely chopped

Coarsely ground white pepper

48 large shrimp, shelled and deveined

Kosher salt

½ cup sherry vinegar

3 tablespoons finely chopped fresh thyme leaves

Whisk together the olive oil, garlic, and white pepper in a large shallow pan or baking dish. Add the shrimp and toss to coat completely. Refrigerate, covered, for 2 hours, no longer.

Preheat a gas or charcoal grill to high.

Remove the shrimp from the marinade and shake off the excess (discard the used marinade). Season with salt and grill until just cooked through, 2 to 3 minutes on each side.

Place on a large platter and immediately drizzle with sherry vinegar and sprinkle with thyme.

Ginger-Marinated Shrimp with Toasted Sesame Seed Vinaigrette

MAKES 8 SERVINGS

This is my version of a dish that you can find in some of the best Asian restaurants. The flavors of fresh ginger, sesame seeds, and sesame oil will make you feel like you are in Asia.

FOR THE TOASTED SESAME SEED VINAIGRETTE:

¼ cup rice wine vinegar

1 tablespoon soy sauce

½ small shallot, coarsely chopped

2 tablespoons toasted sesame seeds (see Note)

1 tablespoon coarsely chopped cilantro

1 tablespoon honey

1 teaspoon sesame oil

½ cup olive oil

Kosher salt and freshly ground pepper

Place the vinegar, soy sauce, shallot, sesame seeds, and cilantro in a blender and blend until smooth. Add the honey. With the motor running, slowly add the sesame and olive oils until emulsified. Season with salt and pepper. May be refrigerated for 1 day; serve at room temperature. Makes about 1 cup.

(continued)

97

FOR THE GINGER-MARINATED SHRIMP:

1 cup olive oil

¼ cup peeled and coarsely chopped gingerroot

3 cloves garlic, coarsely chopped

2 tablespoons soy sauce

48 large shrimp, shelled and deveined

Kosher salt and freshly ground pepper

Toasted Sesame Seed Vinaigrette

2 tablespoons toasted sesame seeds (see Note)

Combine the oil, gingerroot, garlic, and soy sauce in a large shallow baking dish. Add the shrimp and toss to coat. Cover and refrigerate for 1 hour, no longer.

Preheat a gas grill to high or light a hot charcoal fire.

Remove the shrimp from the marinade, shaking off any excess (discard the used marinade). Season with salt and pepper. Grill until just cooked through, 2 to 3 minutes on each side. Arrange on a platter and drizzle with Toasted Sesame Seed Vinaigrette and toasted sesame seeds.

NOTE: To toast sesame seeds, place a heavy, dry skillet over low heat and cook the seeds 2 to 3 minutes, tossing or stirring them so they don't burn. Remove from the heat as soon as they are toasted.

Barbecue Sauce–Soaked Shrimp with Crème Fraîche Dressing

MAKES 8 SERVINGS

A Southern-style dish, rich and delicious, this brings back memories of fabulous dining in New Orleans. If you soak the shrimp in the spicy sauce and then grill them, they will absorb all the complex barbecue flavors.

FOR THE CRÈME FRAÎCHE DRESSING:

2 cups crème fraîche (see Note), or sour cream
2 tablespoons finely chopped red onion
2 cloves garlic, finely chopped
2 tablespoons fresh lime juice
¼ cup finely chopped cilantro
Kosher salt and freshly ground pepper

Combine the crème fraîche, onion, garlic, lime juice, and cilantro in a medium bowl and season with salt and pepper. May be refrigerated, covered, for 1 day. Makes about 2¼ cups.

FOR THE SHRIMP:

2 cups Mesa Barbecue Sauce (page 29)
48 large shrimp, shelled and deveined
Kosher salt and freshly ground pepper
Crème Fraîche Dressing

(continued)

Preheat a gas or charcoal grill to high.

Combine the shrimp and barbecue sauce in a large bowl and refrigerate, covered, for 30 minutes, no longer. Remove the shrimp from the sauce, season with salt and pepper, and grill until cooked through, 2 to 3 minutes on each side (discard the used marinade).

Pile the shrimp on a large platter and serve accompanied by the Crème Fraîche Dressing.

NOTE: To make 2 cups crème fraîche, combine 2 cups heavy cream and 4 tablespoons buttermilk and let sit at room temperature, covered, until thick (from 8 to 24 hours). Can be refrigerated up to 10 days.

Grilled Shrimp Cocktail with Tomato-Horseradish Dipping Sauce

MAKES 8 SERVINGS

Growing up in Manhattan, where it seemed to be a national dish, I've enjoyed shrimp cocktail since early childhood. This one surpasses my memories, with warm, slightly charred shrimp adding the flavor of the grill, and fresh tomatoes and horseradish in the lively sauce.

Although you can make the sauce ahead, I find it easiest to grill the tomatoes for the sauce along with the shrimp, since both require just a few minutes of cooking time. Have the other sauce ingredients in the food processor, throw in the grilled tomatoes, and combine. Then pull the shrimp off the grill and the cocktail is ready to serve.

FOR THE TOMATO-HORSERADISH DIPPING SAUCE:

10 ripe plum tomatoes, halved and seeded

2 tablespoons ketchup

¼ cup freshly grated horseradish or prepared horseradish, drained

2 tablespoons fresh lime juice

2 tablespoons fresh lemon juice

1 tablespoon honey

Dash of Tabasco

2 dashes of Worcestershire sauce

Kosher salt and freshly ground pepper

Preheat a gas or charcoal grill to high.

Grill the tomatoes, turning, just until the skins are lightly charred, 3 to 4 minutes.

(continued)

Place all the ingredients in the bowl of a food processor and process until almost smooth, but with some chunks of tomato remaining. Season with salt and pepper. May be refrigerated for 1 day; serve at room temperature. Makes about 1½ cups.

FOR THE SHRIMP:

½ cup olive oil
4 cloves garlic, coarsely chopped
2 tablespoons finely chopped thyme leaves
48 large shrimp, shelled and deveined
Kosher salt and freshly ground pepper

In a mixing bowl, combine the olive oil, garlic, and thyme. Add the shrimp and refrigerate, covered, for 2 hours, no longer.

Preheat a gas or charcoal grill to high.

Remove the shrimp from the marinade, shaking off any excess (discard the used marinade). Season the shrimp with salt and pepper and grill until golden brown and cooked through, 2 to 3 minutes on each side.

To serve, arrange the shrimp on a large serving platter and accompany with a bowl of the Tomato-Horseradish Dipping Sauce.

Spicy Shrimp with Asian Peanut Dipping Sauce

MAKES 8 SERVINGS

This spicy dish is like a shrimp satay, using peanut butter and Asian flavors to make a great dip for grilled shrimp. Be sure to get the best quality peanut butter.

FOR THE PEANUT DIPPING SAUCE:

¼ cup smooth peanut butter

1 tablespoon peeled and coarsely chopped fresh gingerroot

2 cloves garlic, coarsely chopped

2 tablespoons low-sodium soy sauce

2 tablespoons fresh lime juice

1 tablespoon rice wine vinegar

¾ cup shrimp stock or clam juice

1 teaspoon honey

Kosher salt and freshly ground pepper

¼ cup finely chopped cilantro

¼ cup finely sliced green onion

Combine the peanut butter, gingerroot, garlic, soy sauce, lime juice, vinegar, stock, and honey in a food processor and process until smooth. Season with salt and pepper. Spoon into a medium bowl, fold in the chopped cilantro, and sprinkle the green onion on top. May be refrigerated, covered, for 1 day; serve at room temperature. Makes 2 cups.

(continued)

FOR THE SPICY SHRIMP:

½ cup olive oil

2 tablespoons fresh lime juice

2 chiles de arbol or hot Asian chiles, coarsely chopped

2 tablespoons coarsely chopped fresh gingerroot

6 cloves garlic, coarsely chopped

2 tablespoons coarsely chopped cilantro

48 large shrimp, shelled and deveined

Kosher salt and freshly ground pepper

Combine the oil, lime juice, chiles, gingerroot, garlic, and cilantro in a large shallow pan or baking dish. Add the shrimp and toss to coat. Refrigerate, covered, for 2 hours, no longer.

Preheat a gas or charcoal grill to high.

Remove the shrimp from the marinade, shaking off the excess (discard the used marinade). Grill until just cooked through, 2 to 3 minutes on each side.

To serve, arrange the shrimp on a large serving platter and accompany with a bowl of the Peanut Dipping Sauce.

Shrimp Skewered on Rosemary Branches

MAKES 8 SERVINGS

The perfume of rosemary cooking on the grill will give your dinner a delightful Tuscan feeling. Thread the shrimp on long rosemary branches and serve them that way, hot from the fire.

- 1½ cups olive oil
- 8 cloves garlic, coarsely chopped
- 48 large shrimp, peeled and deveined
- 16 long rosemary branches, soaked in water for 1 hour
- Kosher salt and freshly ground pepper

Combine the olive oil and garlic in a large shallow pan or baking dish. Set aside ½ cup and add shrimp to the pan. Let marinate for 2 hours, no longer.

Preheat a gas or charcoal grill to medium high.

Remove 1 inch of leaves from the bottom of each rosemary branch and with a sharp knife, cut the end of the stem on the bias to make a slight point.

Remove the shrimp from the marinade, shaking off any excess (discard the used marinade). Thread 3 shrimp on each rosemary branch. Season with salt and pepper, and grill until just cooked through, 2 to 3 minutes on each side, basting with the reserved marinade every 30 seconds.

To serve, place the shrimp, still on the rosemary branches on a large platter.

Smoked Chile Butter–Brushed Shrimp with Tomatillo Salsa

MAKES 8 SERVINGS

Compound butter with chipotles (smoked dried jalapeños) adds fiery flavor as it melts into the hot shrimp—brush it on just as you take them off the grill. Chipotles and tart tomatillos have great affinity for each other, which is why this salsa works so well with the dish.

Preparations can all be done ahead and once you're ready to grill, just a few seconds of cooking, and the shrimp are done.

FOR THE SMOKED CHILE BUTTER:

½ pound (2 sticks) unsalted butter, softened
2 chipotle peppers, canned in adobo sauce (see Note)
2 cloves garlic
3 tablespoons coarsely chopped shallots
Juice of 1 lime
Kosher salt and freshly ground pepper

Place the butter, chipotles, garlic, shallots, and lime juice in a food processor and blend until smooth. Season with salt and pepper and place in a small bowl. May be refrigerated, covered, up to 3 days, or frozen; use at room temperature.

FOR THE TOMATILLO SALSA:

10 tomatillos, husked and washed: 5 cut in half, and 5 coarsely chopped
3 tablespoons fresh lime juice
¼ cup finely chopped red onion
1 jalapeño pepper, finely chopped

106

2 tablespoons olive oil

1 teaspoon honey

Kosher salt and freshly ground pepper

¼ cup coarsely chopped cilantro

Place the halved tomatillos and the lime juice in a blender and blend until smooth. Place the coarsely chopped tomatillos, the onion, and the jalapeño in a medium bowl, add the tomatillo mixture, and toss to coat. Add the olive oil and honey and season with salt and pepper. Fold in the cilantro just before serving. May be refrigerated for 1 day without the cilantro; serve at room temperature, with the cilantro added. Makes about 2 cups.

FOR THE SHRIMP:

48 large shrimp, shelled and deveined

Smoked Chile Butter

Kosher salt and freshly ground pepper

Tomatillo Salsa

Preheat a gas or charcoal grill to high.

    Grill the shrimp for 2 to 3 minutes on each side, brushing with the butter every 30 seconds. Season with salt and pepper.

    Remove shrimp to a platter and immediately brush with the remaining butter. Serve the Tomatillo Salsa alongside.

NOTE: Canned chipotle peppers in adobo are available at Hispanic or gourmet markets or from Kitchen Market, 218 Eighth Avenue, New York, NY 10011, 212-243-4433, which has a mail-order list.

Spicy Pineapple-Glazed Sea Scallops with Soy-Miso Vinaigrette and Grilled Pineapple Relish

MAKES 8 SERVINGS

On my first trip to Hawaii, I discovered a luscious combination: sea scallops served with fresh Hawaiian pineapple. Inspired by happy memories, I glazed some sweet scallops with pineapple juice just before grilling, then added a relish of grilled fresh pineapple for good measure.

FOR THE SPICY PINEAPPLE GLAZE:

2 tablespoons olive oil

¼ cup coarsely chopped red onion

2 cloves garlic, coarsely chopped

1 serrano pepper, coarsely chopped

3 cups sweetened pineapple juice

Heat the olive oil in a small saucepan over medium heat until almost smoking. Add the onion and garlic and cook until soft. Add the serrano pepper and pineapple juice, raise the heat to high, and bring the mixture to a boil. Cook until reduced to 1 cup. Place in a blender and blend until smooth. Let cool at room temperature. May be refrigerated, covered, for 1 day; serve at room temperature. Makes about 1¼ cups.

FOR THE GRILLED PINEAPPLE RELISH:

1 large ripe pineapple, peeled, cored,
   and sliced crosswise into 1-inch-thick rings
Vegetable oil for brushing the pineapple
4 green onions (white bulbs and 3 inches of green),
   finely sliced
1 red bell pepper, finely diced
2 tablespoons fresh lime juice
1 jalapeño pepper, finely diced
¼ cup chopped cilantro
1 tablespoon olive oil
Kosher salt and freshly ground pepper

Preheat a gas or charcoal grill to medium high. Brush the pineapple rings with oil on both sides and grill until golden brown and almost cooked through, 3 to 4 minutes on each side. Remove from the grill and chop coarsely.

Place the chopped pineapple in a large bowl, add the green onions, bell pepper, lime juice, jalapeño, cilantro, and oil, and season with salt and pepper. May be refrigerated for 1 day; serve at room temperature. Makes 3 cups.

FOR THE SOY-MISO VINAIGRETTE:

2 tablespoons white miso paste
   (available at Japanese markets)
2 cloves garlic, finely chopped
1 tablespoon peeled and finely chopped gingerroot
3 tablespoons soy sauce
1 tablespoon toasted sesame oil
½ cup peanut oil
1 teaspoon honey
¼ teaspoon freshly ground white pepper

(continued)

109

Whisk all the ingredients together in a small bowl. May be refrigerated, covered, for 1 day; serve at room temperature. Makes about ¾ cup.

FOR THE SCALLOPS:

40 sea scallops, trimmed
Spicy Pineapple Glaze
Grilled Pineapple Relish
Soy-Miso Vinaigrette
Kosher salt and freshly ground pepper

Place the scallops in a large, shallow pan or baking dish, cover with the Pineapple Glaze, and refrigerate, covered, for 30 minutes, no longer.

Preheat a gas or charcoal grill to medium high.

Remove the scallops from the marinade, shaking off any excess (discard the used marinade), season with salt and pepper, and grill until golden and cooked through, 2 to 3 minutes on each side.

Place the Grilled Pineapple Relish in the center of a large platter, arrange the scallops around the relish, and drizzle the scallops with the Soy-Miso Vinaigrette.

Grilled Sea Scallop Ceviche

MAKES 8 SERVINGS

Marinate the scallops to "cook" them in citrus juices and give them that ceviche taste. Then grill them briefly to give them a little color and extra flavor. This dish is a nice first course to serve while the rest of the meal is grilling.

1 cup fresh orange juice

1 cup fresh lime juice

1 cup fresh lemon juice

1 cup olive oil

2 red onions, finely sliced

1 orange, peeled and sectioned

1 lemon, peeled and sectioned

1 lime, peeled and sectioned

2 tablespoons chopped chives

¼ cup coarsely chopped cilantro

32 large sea scallops, halved horizontally
  (this helps the marinade penetrate)

Kosher salt and freshly ground pepper

2 mangoes, peeled and cut into 1-inch cubes

FOR GARNISH:

¼ cup finely chopped chives

¼ cup finely chopped cilantro

In a large bowl, combine the juices, oil, onions, citrus fruits, chives, and cilantro. Add the scallops and refrigerate, covered, 4 to 6 hours.

Preheat a gas or charcoal grill to high.

Remove the scallops from their marinade, shaking off any excess. Strain the marinade, discarding the liquid and herbs, reserving the onions and citrus fruits. Season the scallops with salt and pepper and grill just to mark and heat slightly, about 1 minute on each side. Place on a platter and surround with the reserved onions and citrus fruits and the mango cubes. Garnish with the finely chopped chives and cilantro.

111

Softshell Crab Sandwiches with Basil Pesto Dressing and Jicama Slaw

MAKES 8 SERVINGS

What could be better for lunch at the beach? These sandwiches belong near the water, with jicama slaw on the side for a touch of crispness and sweetness (jicama has the texture of raw potato and the sweetness of apple). Grilling gives the crabs extra crunch, while the inside steams to a buttery softness.

The freshness of basil in the pesto dressing is intoxicating—dress the crabs when they are hot off the grill.

FOR THE BASIL PESTO DRESSING:

½ cup packed basil leaves

2 cloves garlic

1 teaspoon pine nuts

3 tablespoons olive oil

Kosher salt and freshly ground pepper

1½ cups good quality mayonnaise

2 teaspoons fresh lemon juice

Place the basil, garlic, and pine nuts in a food processor and process until smooth. With the motor running, slowly add the olive oil until emulsified. Season with salt and pepper.

In a small bowl, fold the pesto into the mayonnaise, add the lemon juice, and mix until combined. Season with salt and pepper. May be refrigerated for 1 day; serve at room temperature. Makes about 2 cups.

FOR THE JICAMA SLAW:

¼ cup fresh orange juice

2 tablespoons fresh lemon juice

2 tablespoons fresh lime juice

½ shallot, coarsely chopped

2 basil leaves, chiffonade (see Note 1)

½ cup olive oil

1 small jicama, peeled and cut into julienne
   (small matchsticks)

2 large carrots, peeled and grated

2 red bell peppers, seeded and cut into julienne
   (small matchsticks)

1 jalapeño pepper, minced

1 tablespoon honey

Kosher salt

Cayenne

Combine the orange, lemon, and lime juices, the shallot, and the basil in a blender and blend until smooth. With the motor running, slowly add the olive oil until emulsified.

In a medium bowl, combine the jicama, carrots, bell peppers, and jalapeño, and toss with the dressing. Add the honey and season with salt and cayenne.

FOR THE SOFTSHELL CRABS:

8 softshell crabs, cleaned (see Note 2)

Olive oil for brushing the crabs

Kosher salt and freshly ground pepper

8 sourdough rolls, split and most
   of the soft inside scooped out

Jicama Slaw

113

(continued)

Preheat a gas or charcoal grill to medium.

Brush the crabs with olive oil and season with salt and pepper. Grill until crisp and cooked through, about 4 minutes on each side.

For each sandwich, place 1 crab on half a roll and cover with Jicama Slaw. Spread some Basil Pesto Dressing on the remaining half roll and place over the slaw.

NOTES:

1. To cut basil into chiffonade, or fine ribbons, roll up the leaves and cut into thin strips.

2. To clean softshell crabs, use scissors to cut off the eyes and mouth, then lift up the shell on both sides and cut out the spongy gills. Cut off the apron on each crab's underside. Or ask the fishmonger to prepare them.

SAUTÉED SOFTSHELL CRABS WITH LEMON-BROWN BUTTER AND SCOTCH BONNET CHILE

MAKES 8 SERVINGS

Put a pan right on the grate with a little olive oil and let it get very hot, to cook these crabs. You'll get a great sear on the shells, while the meat inside steams. Make a brown butter sauce right in the pan, with fresh lemon juice and a scotch bonnet chile for a little spiciness, and coat the crabs with the buttery sauce.

3 tablespoons olive oil

8 softshell crabs, cleaned (see Note)

2 shallots, finely chopped

½ cup dry white wine

Kosher salt and freshly ground pepper

½ pound (2 sticks) cold unsalted butter, quartered

½ cup fresh lemon juice

1 scotch bonnet chile, finely chopped

¼ cup chopped flat-leaf parsley

Preheat a gas or charcoal grill to high.

Place a large enamel-coated cast-iron or nonreactive skillet on the grill and heat 1½ tablespoons of the oil until almost smoking. Season the crabs on both sides with salt and pepper and sauté 4 crabs until crisp and golden brown, 3 to 4 minutes on each side. Remove the crabs to a platter, heat the remaining 1½ tablespoons of oil in the pan, and repeat with the remaining 4 crabs.

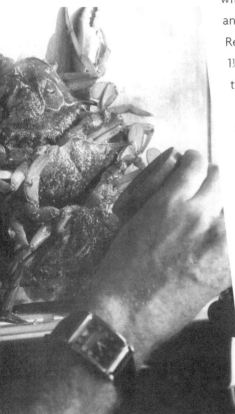

Remove the second batch of crabs, add the shallots to the pan, and cook until soft. Add the wine and reduce until dry. Add the butter to the skillet and cook until it just begins to turn brown, being careful that it does not burn. Add the lemon juice and chile and season with salt and pepper. Remove from the heat, add the parsley, and pour over the crabs. Serve immediately.

NOTE: To clean softshell crabs, use scissors to cut off the eyes and mouth, then lift up the shell on both sides and cut out the spongy gills. Cut off the apron on each crab's underside. Or ask the fishmonger to prepare them.

115

Whole Lobster Smothered in Cascabel Chile Butter

MAKES 8 SERVINGS

This is awesome! To make preparation easier, boil the whole lobsters ahead of time without cooking them all the way through, and let them get cold. When your guests are ready for dinner, cut the lobsters right down the middle and put them on the grill, where they will pick up that smoky grill flavor. Let the Cascabel Chile Butter come to room temperature so it's nice and soft. Then take the hot lobster off the grill and stick it right into the butter, or spread the butter all over it with a big brush, so it's drowning in butter.

FOR THE CASCABEL CHILE BUTTER:

> 2 tablespoons olive oil
> ¼ cup finely chopped red onion
> 2 teaspoons cascabel chile powder (see Note), or any good quality chile powder
> 2 tablespoons fresh lime juice
> 1 pound (4 sticks) unsalted butter, softened
> Kosher salt and freshly ground pepper

Heat the olive oil until almost smoking in a small saucepan over medium heat, and cook the onion until soft. Add the cascabel chile powder and cook for 1 minute. Let cool to room temperature. Place the onion mixture, lime juice, and butter in a food processor and blend until smooth. Season with salt and pepper and place in a small bowl. May be refrigerated, covered, up to 3 days, or frozen; use at room temperature.

FOR THE LOBSTERS:

8 live lobsters, 2 to 3 pounds each
Olive oil for brushing the lobsters
Kosher salt and freshly ground pepper

In a large pot of boiling salted water (or use several pots), cook 1 or 2 lobsters at a time until they are three-quarters done. A 2-pound lobster should take about 11 minutes and a 3-pound lobster should take 18 to 19 minutes. Let the lobsters cool to room temperature and then refrigerate them for up to 1 day.

To finish the lobsters, preheat a gas or charcoal grill to high. Split the lobsters in half, brush with olive oil, season with salt and pepper, and grill flesh-side down until nicely marked, 2 to 3 minutes. Turn over and grill shell-side down for another minute.

To serve, brush the hot lobsters with Cascabel Chile Butter and place on several large platters.

NOTE: Cascabel chile powder is available at Hispanic or gourmet markets, or from Kitchen Market, 218 Eighth Avenue, New York, NY 10011, 212-243-4433, which has a mail-order list.

117

Lobster Tails with Curry-Mango Butter

MAKES 8 SERVINGS

On a little island off Anguilla, there is a restaurant where they serve grilled lobster tails with curry butter. As you get off the boat and walk onto the island, you can smell the fantastic aromas of the lobster as it comes off the grill and the curry butter melting into it. I went back again and again—it was irresistible. For my version, I've added the sweetness of fresh mango.

FOR THE CURRY-MANGO BUTTER:

2 tablespoons olive oil

1 small onion, finely chopped

2 tablespoons good quality curry powder

1 teaspoon ancho chile powder (see Note),
     or good quality chile powder

1 mango, peeled, pitted, and pureed

2 tablespoons fresh lime juice

½ pound (2 sticks) unsalted butter, softened

Kosher salt and freshly ground pepper

Heat the olive oil in a small saucepan over medium heat until almost smoking and cook the onion until softened, 4 to 5 minutes. Add the curry and ancho powders, lower the heat, and cook for 5 minutes, stirring constantly. Add the mango puree and lime juice, and cook an additional 15 to 20 minutes, stirring often. Let cool at room temperature.

In a food processor, combine the mango mixture and the butter and process until smooth. Season with salt and pepper.

Place a sheet of parchment or wax paper on a work surface. Form the butter into a roll about 1 inch in diameter and place it along the long side of the paper, leaving a border of 1 inch. Roll up the butter in the paper and refrigerate for 30 minutes or up to 3 days. The butter may also be frozen.

FOR THE LOBSTER TAILS:

16 lobster tails
Olive oil for brushing the lobster tails
Kosher salt and freshly ground pepper
Curry-Mango Butter

Preheat a gas or charcoal grill to high.

Brush the lobster tails with olive oil and season with salt and pepper. Grill flesh-side down until cooked through, 4 to 5 minutes; turn and grill on the shell side another 2 to 3 minutes.

Place the lobster tails on a serving platter and top each with a slice of Curry-Mango Butter.

NOTE: Ancho chile powder is available at Hispanic or gourmet markets, or from Kitchen Market, 218 Eighth Avenue, New York, NY 10011, 212-243-4433, which has a mail-order list.

Lobster Rolls with Curried Mayonnaise

MAKES 8 SERVINGS

Every beach town in America seems to have its own favorite restaurant for lobster rolls, usually a modest little place on the side of the road. My take on this all-American sandwich adds Curried Mayonnaise for extra flavor.

FOR THE CURRIED MAYONNAISE:

2 tablespoons olive oil

½ cup coarsely chopped Spanish onion

2 cloves garlic, coarsely chopped

2 tablespoons good quality curry powder

2 cups good quality mayonnaise

2 tablespoons fresh lime juice

Kosher salt and freshly ground pepper

Heat the olive oil until almost smoking in a small saucepan over medium heat and cook the onion and garlic until soft, 3 to 4 minutes. Add the curry powder and cook, stirring constantly until the flavors mellow, 15 to 20 minutes. Remove from the heat and let cool to room temperature.

Combine the curry mixture, mayonnaise, and lime juice in a food processor and blend until smooth. Season with salt and pepper. May be refrigerated, covered, for 1 day. Makes about 2 cups.

FOR THE LOBSTER ROLLS:

4 cups grilled lobster meat, from four 2- to 3-pound lobsters
(see Whole Lobster Smothered in Cascabel Chile Butter,
page 116, or use any cooked lobster meat)

1 medium stalk celery, cut in ¼-inch-thick slices

¼ cup finely diced red bell pepper

¼ cup finely chopped red onion

2 cups Curried Mayonnaise

¼ cup coarsely chopped cilantro

Kosher salt and freshly ground pepper

8 hot dog or hamburger rolls

Olive oil for brushing the rolls

Combine the lobster, celery, bell pepper, onion, mayonnaise, and cilantro in a large bowl and season with salt and pepper.

Split the rolls and brush with olive oil. Grill, split-side down, until golden, about 30 seconds.

Fill the rolls with the lobster salad and arrange on a serving platter.

121

Grilled Lobster Quesadillas with Yellow Tomato–Roasted Garlic Salsa

MAKES 8 SERVINGS

This dish is turning into a Mesa Grill classic, and it's really simple to do, especially if you've made lobster for a lot of people and you have some leftovers. I got the idea for combining lobster with toasted garlic when I tried Lydia Shire's lobster pizza at Biba in Boston. The two flavors really work well together, even without the pizza.

FOR THE YELLOW TOMATO–ROASTED GARLIC SALSA:

3 ripe yellow tomatoes, coarsely chopped

4 cloves roasted garlic, finely chopped (see Note 1)

2 tablespoons finely diced red onion

½ serrano pepper, finely diced

1 tablespoon rice wine vinegar

1 tablespoon coarsely chopped fresh thyme leaves

Kosher salt and freshly ground pepper

Combine the tomatoes, garlic, onion, serrano pepper, vinegar, and thyme in a medium bowl and season with salt and pepper. May be refrigerated, covered, for 1 day; serve at room temperature. Makes a little over 1 cup.

FOR THE LOBSTER:

Twelve 6-inch flour tortillas (or cut 8-inch tortillas to size, using a 6-inch plate as a guide)

1¼ cups grated Monterey Jack cheese

1¼ cups grated white Cheddar

1 lobster (2½ pounds) grilled, meat removed, and coarsely chopped (see Whole Lobster Smothered in Cascabel Chile Butter, page 116, or use any cooked lobster meat)

1 large red onion, thinly sliced

1 head roasted garlic, peeled and finely chopped

2 jalapeño peppers, seeded and coarsely chopped

¼ cup finely chopped cilantro

Olive oil for brushing the tortillas

1½ tablespoons ancho chile powder (see Note 2)

Yellow Tomato–Roasted Garlic Salsa

Preheat a gas or charcoal grill to low to medium.

Place 8 tortillas on a work surface. Divide the cheeses, lobster meat, red onion, garlic, jalapeños, and cilantro among the tortillas. Stack half of the tortillas on top of the remaining half, to make four 2-layer quesadillas. Top with a final layer of tortillas, brush with oil, and sprinkle with chile powder. Grill oiled-side down until golden brown, 3 to 4 minutes. Brush with oil, sprinkle with chile powder, turn, and grill until the other side is golden brown and the cheese has melted.

Place the quesadillas on a large platter, cut each into 4 wedges, and garnish with the Yellow Tomato–Roasted Garlic Salsa.

NOTES:

1. To oven-roast a head of garlic, first cut off the top. Rub the garlic with olive oil and sprinkle with salt and pepper, wrap it in foil, place it on a baking sheet, and roast at 300°F until soft, about 45 minutes.

2. Ancho chile powder is available at Hispanic or gourmet markets, or from Kitchen Market, 218 Eighth Avenue, New York, NY 10011, 212-243-4433, which has a mail-order list.

123

Paella on the Grill

Paella is a magnificent dish for feeding a lot of people. You can grill all the ingredients ahead of time and cook the saffron rice ahead, as well. When the guests arrive, heat a big, sturdy pan on top of the grill and put the rice in there with the grilled fish and chicken, add the Lemon Aioli, and mix them all together. Season it up, get it nice and hot, and serve it—boom—from the grill to the table.

Organization is crucial to this dish!

For preparing all components of the recipe, except the Lemon Aioli, preheat the grill, side burner, or stove to medium high.

FOR THE LEMON AIOLI:

1 cup good quality mayonnaise
4 cloves garlic, minced
¼ cup fresh lemon juice
1 tablespoon chopped lemon zest
Kosher salt and freshly ground pepper

Combine the mayonnaise, garlic, lemon juice, and lemon zest in a small bowl and season with salt and pepper. May be refrigerated for 1 day. Makes 1 cup.

FOR THE RICE:

3 tablespoons olive oil
½ pound chorizo, thinly sliced
2 medium onions, finely chopped
4 cups converted white rice
1 tablespoon saffron threads
8 cups water
Kosher salt and freshly ground pepper

124

On the gas or charcoal grill, or the side burner (or stove), heat the oil in a large saucepan until almost smoking and cook the chorizo until browned and the fat has rendered. Remove the chorizo to a paper towel–lined plate. Pour off all but 2 table-spoons of the fat, add the onions to the pan, and cook until translucent, 4 to 5 minutes. Add the rice and stir until coated with the oil.

Combine the saffron and the water, let sit 1 minute, and add to the rice. Add the chorizo, season with salt and pepper, stir, cover, and cook until the rice is al dente, 12 to 15 minutes.

FOR THE CHICKEN:

8 chicken thighs
Olive oil for brushing
Kosher salt and freshly ground pepper

Brush the chicken thighs on both sides with olive oil and season with salt and pep-per. On a gas or charcoal grill, cook the chicken skin-side down until golden brown, about 5 minutes. Turn over and continue cooking for 6 minutes; turn again and grill until cooked through, an additional 4 minutes.

FOR THE MUSSELS AND CLAMS:

16 littleneck clams, scrubbed
24 cultivated mussels, cleaned
   (cultivated mussels don't have to be debearded)
Kosher salt and freshly ground pepper

On the gas or charcoal grill, or the side burner (or stove), heat 1 inch of water in a large stockpot until simmering. Add the clams, cover, and cook 4 minutes. Add the mussels, cover, and cook an additional 6 to 7 minutes, until the clams and mussels have opened, discarding any that do not open. Season with salt and pepper, remove from the heat, and keep covered.

(continued)

FOR THE SEA SCALLOPS AND SHRIMP:

8 large sea scallops

8 large shrimp

¼ cup olive oil

Kosher salt and freshly ground pepper

Brush the scallops and shrimp with olive oil on both sides and season with salt and pepper. On the gas or charcoal grill, cook them until golden brown, 1 to 2 minutes on each side.

FOR THE LOBSTER:

2 whole lobsters, about 1½ pounds each, steamed and split in half (see Whole Lobster Smothered in Cascabel Chile Butter, page 116)

3 tablespoons olive oil

Kosher salt and freshly ground pepper

Remove the lobster claws, pull or cut off the tails and cut in half lengthwise, and discard the bodies. Brush the lobster pieces on both sides with olive oil and season with salt and pepper. Grill for 3 minutes on the flesh side; turn and grill for 1 minute.

FOR THE GRILLED VEGETABLES:

32 asparagus spears, trimmed

8 ripe plum tomatoes, halved

¼ cup olive oil

¼ cup honey

Kosher salt and freshly ground pepper

Brush the asparagus and tomatoes with olive oil and honey and season with salt and pepper. Grill until marked but not cooked through, 2 to 3 minutes on each side.

TO ASSEMBLE THE PAELLA:

½ cup coarsely chopped flat-leaf parsley

Add the chicken, mussels, clams, scallops, shrimp, lobster, and vegetables to the rice. Fold in the Lemon Aioli and stir to combine. Cook over medium heat on the grill or side burner (or stove) for 5 minutes to allow the flavors to meld. Season with salt and pepper. Spoon onto a large platter and garnish with chopped parsley.

127

STEAMED LITTLENECK CLAMS WITH CHORIZO AND FRESH CORN

MAKES 8 SERVINGS

My guests get to enjoy steamed clams before they start their main course, sometimes done this way and sometimes in Green Chile–Coconut Milk Broth. Try to get small clams, like littlenecks. With clams, remember that the smaller, the sweeter. For either recipe, just put them and the other flavorful ingredients in a heavy saucepan and let them open right on the fire. Set out bowls of steaming clams around the grill and people will come over and join you while you cook—that's what I like to do.

1 pound Spanish chorizo links
2 tablespoons olive oil
1 Spanish onion, finely chopped
4 cloves garlic, finely chopped
1 cup dry white wine
80 littleneck clams, scrubbed well
2 cups fresh corn kernels (4 ears; see Note)
¼ cup finely chopped flat-leaf parsley
Kosher salt and freshly ground pepper

Preheat a gas or charcoal grill to medium high.

Grill the chorizo just to obtain grill marks and heat through, 2 to 3 minutes on each side. (Spanish chorizo is cured and so requires only short cooking.) Remove from the grill and let sit 5 minutes. Slice on the bias into ¼-inch-thick slices.

In a large, enamel-coated Dutch oven, heat the oil over medium-high heat, using the side burners or the grill. Add the onion and garlic, and cook until lightly golden, 5 to 6 minutes. Add the wine and reduce completely. Add the clams, cover the pot, and cook until all the clams open, 10 to 12 minutes. During the last 5 minutes of cooking, add the chorizo and the corn. Discard any clams that have not opened.

Remove from the heat, add the parsley, and season with salt and pepper. Pour into a large bowl and serve with Grilled Bread with Roasted Garlic Butter and Fresh Herbs (page 28).

NOTE: To remove corn kernels, stand each ear on a cutting surface and scrape downward with a sharp knife.

129

Littleneck Clams Steamed in Green Chile–Coconut Milk Broth

MAKES 8 SERVINGS

Here is another way to steam sweet littlenecks on the grill, this time in a complex broth that flavors them with layer upon layer of spicy, sweet, tropical notes.

2 tablespoons olive oil

1 large red onion, coarsely chopped

6 cloves garlic, coarsely chopped

2 tablespoons peeled and coarsely chopped fresh gingerroot

1 cup dry white wine

2 cups clam juice

1 can (14 ounces) unsweetened coconut milk

2 poblano peppers, grilled (see Note) and coarsely chopped

1 serrano or jalapeño pepper, coarsely chopped

½ cup packed spinach leaves

½ cup water

1 tablespoon honey

Kosher salt and freshly ground pepper

80 littleneck clams, scrubbed

Preheat a gas or charcoal grill to medium high, or use a side burner (or the stove).

Heat the oil in a large, enamel-coated Dutch oven until almost smoking and cook the onion until soft, 4 to 5 minutes. Add the garlic and gingerroot and cook for 2 minutes. Add the wine and reduce until almost dry. Add the clam juice, coconut milk, poblanos, and serrano or jalapeño, and bring to a boil. Add the spinach leaves and cook until just wilted, 1 to 2 minutes.

Transfer the mixture to a blender, add water, and blend until smooth. Return the mixture to the pot and bring to a boil. Add the honey, and season with salt and pepper. Add the clams, stir, cover, and place on the grill. Cover the grill and cook until all the clams open, 10 to 12 minutes. Discard any clams that do not open.

To serve, pour the clams and their broth into a large bowl.

NOTE: To grill poblanos, brush with olive oil and season with salt and pepper. Grill over high heat until charred on all sides. Place in a bowl, cover with plastic wrap, and let sit for 15 minutes. Then peel, halve, and seed.

131

Squid with Avocado-Tomato Salad and Smoked Chile Dressing

MAKES 8 SERVINGS

This salad is based on classic Mesa flavors—chipotle peppers, avocados, and tomatoes—and it is something like our popular Avocado-Tomato Salsa. Barely mix the avocados and tomatoes, so they don't become mushy.

Grill squid whole and do it very quickly, before it has a chance to turn rubbery. Then pull it off the grill and slice it.

FOR THE SMOKED CHILE DRESSING:

¼ cup red wine vinegar

1 chipotle pepper

2 cloves garlic

¼ cup cilantro leaves

½ cup olive oil

1 tablespoon honey

Kosher salt

Place the vinegar, chipotle, garlic, and cilantro in a blender and blend until smooth. With the motor running, slowly add the olive oil until emulsified. Season with honey and salt. May be refrigerated for 1 day; serve at room temperature.

FOR THE SQUID:

16 whole squid, skinned and cleaned (have your fishmonger do this, or purchase cleaned squid)

Olive oil for brushing the squid

Kosher salt and freshly ground pepper

Preheat a gas or charcoal grill to high.

Brush the squid with olive oil and season with salt and pepper. Grill until just cooked, 1½ to 2 minutes on each side.

Remove from the grill and let sit until cool enough to handle. Slice into ½-inch-thick rings.

FOR THE AVOCADO-TOMATO SALAD:

4 ripe avocados, peeled, pitted, and cut into ½-inch dice

4 ripe plum tomatoes, finely diced

¼ cup finely diced red onion

1 small jalapeño pepper, finely chopped

3 tablespoons coarsely chopped cilantro

3 tablespoons mint, chiffonade (see Note)

¼ cup fresh lime juice

Kosher salt and freshly ground pepper

6 cups mesclun greens

Smoked Chile Dressing

In a medium bowl, carefully combine the avocados, tomatoes, onion, jalapeño, cilantro, mint, lime juice, salt, and pepper. In another bowl, toss the greens with a few tablespoons of the Smoked Chile Dressing.

Arrange the greens on a large serving platter. Mound the avocado salad in the middle and arrange the squid around the avocado. Drizzle with the remaining dressing.

NOTE: To cut mint into chiffonade, or fine ribbons, roll up the leaves and cut into thin strips.

133

Squid with Grilled Tomato–Bread Salad

MAKES 8 SERVINGS

The grill offers an imaginative way to use day-old bread, which happens to be very good. Many cultures have a bread salad recipe, among them France, Tuscany, and our own American South, but here it is transformed by Southwestern flavors.

While the grill is hot, quickly grill both the squid and the bread for the salad.

FOR THE SQUID:

16 whole squid, skinned and cleaned (have your fishmonger do this, or purchase cleaned squid)

Olive oil for brushing the squid

Kosher salt and freshly ground pepper

Preheat a gas or charcoal grill to high.

Brush the squid with olive oil and season with salt and pepper. Grill until just cooked, 1½ to 2 minutes on each side. Remove from the grill and let sit until cool enough to handle. Slice into ½-inch-thick rings.

FOR THE SALAD:

½ cup red wine vinegar

1 tablespoon honey

1 tablespoon pureed canned chipotle peppers in adobo (see Note)

½ cup olive oil, plus extra for brushing the bread, tomatoes, and red onion

12 slices (½ inch thick) day-old Italian bread

4 large tomatoes, halved and seeded

1 large red onion, sliced ¼ inch thick

Kosher salt and freshly ground pepper

Grilled squid

¼ cup coarsely chopped cilantro

In a small bowl, whisk together the vinegar, honey, chipotle puree, and ½ cup of olive oil. Season with salt and pepper.

Brush the bread, tomatoes, and red onion with olive oil and season with salt and pepper. Grill the bread until golden brown on both sides, about 2 minutes total. Grill the tomatoes and onion, turning, until golden brown and just cooked through, 5 to 6 minutes.

Cut the bread into ½-inch cubes. Coarsely chop the tomatoes and onion.

Place the bread, tomatoes, and onion in a medium bowl, pour the vinaigrette over them, and stir well to combine. Let sit for 15 minutes.

Arrange the bread mixture on a platter, top with the grilled squid, and sprinkle with the cilantro.

NOTE: Canned chipotle peppers in adobo are available at Hispanic or gourmet markets, or from Kitchen Market, 218 Eighth Avenue, New York, NY 10011, 212-243-4433, which has a mail-order list.

To make chipotle puree, process canned chipotles in a blender or food processor, along with a little of their liquid.

135

GRILLED SQUID SALAD WITH PAPAYA, GREEN ONIONS, AND PEANUTS

MAKES 8 SERVINGS

This Asian-influenced dish is perfect as an appetizer—let your guests walk around with a plateful while you're grilling the main course. Since it's light, grilled squid is a healthful departure from fried calamari.

When squid is grilled very quickly, the texture is perfect, never rubbery. Grill it whole and cut it into rings after it's done.

FOR THE GRILLED SQUID:

16 whole squid, skinned and cleaned (have your fishmonger do this, or purchase cleaned squid)

Olive oil for brushing the squid

Kosher salt and freshly ground pepper

Preheat a gas or charcoal grill to high.

Brush the squid with olive oil and season with salt and pepper. Grill until just cooked, 1½ to 2 minutes on each side.

Remove from the grill and let sit until cool enough to handle. Slice into ½-inch-thick rings.

FOR THE PAPAYA–GREEN ONION SALAD:

2 tablespoons fresh lemon juice

2 tablespoons fresh lime juice

1 tablespoon soy sauce

¼ cup olive oil

1 small jalapeño pepper, finely diced

1 pound arugula, washed well

2 ripe papayas, peeled, pitted, and thinly sliced

4 green onions (white bulbs and 3 inches of green),
    finely sliced

Grilled squid

½ cup coarsely chopped peanuts

2 tablespoons finely chopped cilantro

In a small bowl, whisk together the lemon and lime juices, soy sauce, olive oil, and jalapeño until combined.

Arrange the arugula on a large platter, and top with the papaya and green onion. Mound the squid in the center of the platter. Drizzle everything with the vinaigrette and sprinkle with the peanuts and cilantro.

FINS AND SHELLS

5. BEEF, LAMB, PORK, AND RIBS

There are times in life when nothing but a thick, charred, juicy steak hot from the fire qualifies as real food. Simplicity is the whole thing in grilling steaks: just leave them alone (don't keep moving them) and they will develop a rich, dark crust. But since red meat is dense and can take a lot of flavoring, steaks will take well to a spice rub or an herbal coating. And filet mignon, which has terrific buttery texture but is less tasty than other steaks, responds to the enhancement of a black pepper and molasses marinade. Whether they are spiced beforehand or not, serve steaks with accompaniments that add even more flavor and heat, such as Mesa Barbecue Sauce or Tamarind Barbecue Sauce.

A heavy pan right on top of the grill is a good thing to use when you want to cook steak and save its juices for a delicious pan sauce. When the steak is done, add mustard and honey to the pan and swirl everything around over the fire, bringing up the smoky cooked-on bits from the bottom, and pour the juices over the sizzling meat.

Dense lamb cooks best over low heat. You want it to cook slowly, forming a crusty outside surface without burning. The juicy meat is delicious in tacos with Tomato-Mint Relish, or in a salad with crisp chicory, sweet avocados, and ripe nectarines. If you have always loved the traditional combination of lamb chops and mint, try my version, with a blast of habañero lighting up the mint glaze. Or brush thick chops with a Mustard-Molasses Glaze, for a sweet and spicy crust.

Grill pork chops under a glaze that combines the sharpness of horseradish and the mellow sweetness of maple syrup, or marinate in hoisin sauce or a combination of orange, ginger, and paprika. Pork loin sliced thin and grilled makes a sensational sandwich when combined with grilled bell peppers and Spicy Mango Ketchup.

Ribs can be tricky because they have to cook for a long time. Do them really slowly on the grill, being very careful and tending them as they turn dark and crusty. Brushed with a sweet and spicy sauce or glazed with apricots and fresh mint, they are supremely tender, with a caramelized outside and that smoky grill flavor.

RECIPES

Bobby's Dry-Rubbed Rib-Eye Steaks with Mesa Barbecue Sauce

Porterhouse Steak with Tamarind Barbecue Sauce and Basil-Marinated Tomatoes

Beef Tenderloin with Yogurt Sauce and Tomato-Garlic Relish

Beef Tenderloin Crusted with Cumin and Fresh Garlic

Rib-Eye Steak with Chimichurri Marinade and Dried Chile–Mustard Sauce

Pan-Seared Porterhouse Steaks with Honey-Mustard Pan Juice

Black Pepper and Molasses-Glazed Filet Mignon

Grilled Steak Salad with Poblano Vinaigrette

Moroccan Spice–Rubbed Leg of Lamb with Apricot Chutney

Lamb and Red Onion Tacos with Tomato-Mint Relish

Tarragon-Marinated Lamb Chops with Pineapple-Pecan Relish

Lamb Chops with Habañero-Mint Glaze

Lamb Chops with Mustard-Molasses Glaze

Loin of Lamb Rubbed with Garlic and Cumin with Grilled Lemons, Yogurt Sauce, and Grilled Pita

Pork Chops with Horseradish-Maple Glaze

Hoisin-Marinated Pork Chops with Pineapple–Green Onion Relish

Pork Chops Marinated in Orange, Ginger, and Toasted Paprika

Grilled Pork Loin Sandwiches with Spicy Mango Ketchup

Grilled Mozzarella and Black Pepper Quesadilla with Prosciutto di Parma

Spicy Barbecued Ribs with Peanut–Green Onion Relish

Slow-Grilled Pork Ribs Basted with Dried Apricot and Fresh Mint Barbecue Glaze

Indian-Spiced Barbecued Ribs

Bobby's Dry-Rubbed Rib-Eye Steaks with Mesa Barbecue Sauce

MAKES 8 SERVINGS

FOR BOBBY'S DRY RUB:

¼ cup paprika

1 cup ancho chile powder

1 tablespoon ground cumin

1 tablespoon ground coriander

1 teaspoon cayenne

2 teaspoons dry mustard

2 teaspoons dried oregano

1 tablespoon kosher salt

1 teaspoon freshly ground black pepper

Combine all the ingredients in a small bowl. Makes about 1¼ cups. Any extra will keep in a tightly covered glass jar for several months.

FOR THE STEAKS:

8 rib-eye steaks (10 ounces each)

1 cup Bobby's Dry Rub

Olive oil for brushing the steaks

2 cups Mesa Barbecue Sauce (page 29)

Preheat a gas or charcoal grill to high. Rub each steak on one side with the dry rub, brush with olive oil, and grill, rub-side down, until golden brown, 3 to 4 minutes. Turn over and continue grilling 4 to 5 minutes for medium rare. Place on a large serving platter and brush with Mesa Barbecue Sauce.

141

Porterhouse Steak with Tamarind Barbecue Sauce and Basil-Marinated Tomatoes

MAKES 8 SERVINGS

For Basil-Marinated Tomatoes, take the best tomatoes and basil of the season and flavor them with vinegar, olive oil, and freshly cracked black pepper. This is a great condiment to go with steak, and something I made at Miracle Grill a long time ago. It's one of those things that never dies.

Tamarind, which comes from an Indian datelike fruit, has a tart, tangy flavor and gives another dimension to barbecue sauce.

FOR THE TAMARIND BARBECUE SAUCE:

2 tablespoons unsalted butter

½ cup finely diced onion

2 cloves garlic, finely diced

8 canned plum tomatoes, coarsely chopped

¼ cup ketchup

¼ cup water

2 tablespoons Dijon mustard

2 tablespoons dark brown sugar

3 tablespoons molasses

2 tablespoons tamarind concentrate or paste

1 teaspoon cayenne

1 tablespoon ancho chile powder, or good quality chile powder

1 tablespoon paprika

Kosher salt and freshly ground pepper

Melt the butter in a large saucepan over medium-high heat, add the onion and garlic, and cook until soft, 3 or 4 minutes. Add the tomatoes, ketchup, water, mustard, sugar, molasses, tamarind concentrate, cayenne, ancho chile powder, paprika, salt, and pepper, and cook for an additional 15 minutes. Place the mixture in a blender and blend until smooth. Return to the saucepan and cook over medium-high heat until thickened, about 20 minutes. May be refrigerated for 1 day; serve at room temperature. Makes about 4 cups.

FOR THE BASIL-MARINATED TOMATOES:

4 cups cherry tomatoes, halved
¼ cup basil chiffonade
3 tablespoons olive oil
¼ cup balsamic vinegar
Kosher salt and freshly cracked black pepper

Combine the tomatoes, basil, olive oil, and vinegar in a medium bowl and season with salt and pepper. May be refrigerated for 1 day; serve at room temperature. Makes about 4 cups.

FOR THE STEAKS:

8 porterhouse steaks (about 10 ounces each)
Olive oil for brushing the steaks
Kosher salt and freshly ground pepper
Tamarind Barbecue Sauce

Preheat a gas or charcoal grill to high. Brush the steaks with oil, and season with salt and pepper on both sides. Grill the steaks 5 to 6 minutes on each side for medium rare. During the last 2 minutes of cooking, brush them with the Tamarind Barbecue Sauce and grill for 1 minute on each side. Remove from the grill, brush again with the sauce, and place on a large serving platter. Serve the Basil-Marinated Tomatoes and any extra sauce alongside.

143

Beef Tenderloin with Yogurt Sauce and Tomato-Garlic Relish

MAKES 8 SERVINGS

Tomato-Garlic Relish adds spice to this Mediterranean-style dish and yogurt cools it down. Wrap slices of the grilled tenderloin in a pita, for a great casual sandwich.

FOR THE TOMATO-GARLIC RELISH:

4 large ripe tomatoes, seeded and finely diced

2 cloves garlic, finely chopped

½ cup finely sliced red onion

2 jalapeño or serrano peppers, finely diced

1 teaspoon hot paprika or cayenne

2 tablespoons olive oil

2 tablespoons fresh lemon juice

Kosher salt and freshly ground pepper

Combine the tomatoes, garlic, onion, peppers, paprika, olive oil, and lemon juice in a medium bowl and season with salt and pepper. May be refrigerated for 1 day; serve at room temperature. Makes about 2½ cups.

FOR THE YOGURT SAUCE:

2 cups plain yogurt, drained (see Note)

½ cup peeled and finely diced cucumbers

4 cloves garlic, finely chopped

2 tablespoons fresh lemon juice

1 teaspoon cumin

Kosher salt and freshly ground pepper

2 tablespoons finely chopped cilantro

144

Combine the drained yogurt, cucumbers, garlic, lemon juice, and cumin in a small bowl and season with salt and pepper. Refrigerate, covered, for 2 hours or overnight. Add the cilantro just before serving. Makes about 2½ cups.

FOR THE BEEF:

Two beef tenderloins (about 2 pounds each)
¼ cup olive oil, plus extra for brushing the pitas
4 cloves garlic, coarsely chopped
Kosher salt and freshly ground pepper
8 pocketless pita breads
2 cups arugula

Whisk together the oil and garlic in a medium-size shallow baking dish, add the tenderloins, and turn to coat well. Refrigerate, covered, for 1 to 8 hours.

Preheat a gas or charcoal grill to high.

Remove the meat from the marinade and shake off the excess (discard the used marinade). Season with salt and pepper. Grill until medium rare, 5 to 6 minutes on each side, remove from the grill, and let sit 10 minutes.

Brush the pitas with olive oil and grill 10 seconds on each side. Let rest 10 minutes.

Slice the beef ¼ inch thick. Divide among the grilled pitas, top with arugula and Tomato-Garlic Relish, and fold in half to enclose the filling. Arrange on a large serving platter and serve with the Yogurt Sauce on the side.

NOTE: To drain yogurt, place it in a cheesecloth-lined strainer over a bowl for 1 hour, until thickened. Discard the liquid that remains in the bowl.

BEEF, LAMB, PORK, AND RIBS

Beef Tenderloin Crusted with Cumin and Fresh Garlic

MAKES 8 SERVINGS

Cumin and garlic are two strong flavors that go in opposite directions, but when you put them together they cooperate and give tenderloin a Cuban or Latin-American touch. The cumin provides a spicy crust.

¼ cup olive oil

2 tablespoons ground cumin

8 cloves garlic, smashed

2 tablespoons fresh lime juice

2 tablespoons coarsely chopped cilantro

¼ teaspoon coarsely ground black pepper

2 beef tenderloins (about 2 pounds each)

Kosher salt

Place the oil, cumin, garlic, lime juice, cilantro, and pepper in a food processor and process to a smooth paste. Place the tenderloins in a large shallow baking dish or pan and cover with the marinade, rubbing it into the meat. Refrigerate, covered, for 4 hours or overnight.

Preheat a gas or charcoal grill to medium high.

Remove the tenderloins from the dish; do *not* wipe off the excess marinade. Season with salt and grill until medium rare, 5 minutes on each side. Remove from the grill and let rest 5 minutes. Slice on the bias, ½ inch thick, and arrange on a serving platter.

146

Rib-Eye Steak with Chimichurri Marinade and Dried Chile–Mustard Sauce

MAKES 8 SERVINGS

When I go to a restaurant, the steak I love to order is rib-eye. I know it's marbled with fat, but the truth is, that's where all the flavor lies. A rib-eye makes for a more interesting meal than, say, a shell steak because it combines different textures and flavors into a single cut of meat. It has a chewy, beefy outside, as well as a tender inside loin, so it's never boring.

Chimichurri, the Argentine marinade, is well suited to a steak like rib-eye. It's garlic based, with a very green, herbaceous taste that comes from lots of parsley, cilantro, and oregano, plus it has the kick of jalapeños and ancho chile powder.

FOR THE DRIED CHILE–MUSTARD SAUCE:

> **2 cups Dijon mustard**
> **¼ cup whole grain mustard**
> **3 tablespoons ancho chile powder (see Note)**
> **3 tablespoons warm water**

Place all the ingredients in a small bowl and mix well. Makes about 1¼ cups. May be refrigerated for 1 day; serve at room temperature.

(continued)

147

FOR THE CHIMICHURRI MARINADE:

6 cloves garlic

3 fresh bay leaves (dry may be substituted, but be sure to
    strain out any that do not get blended)

2 jalapeño peppers, coarsely chopped

1 tablespoon kosher salt

¼ cup white wine vinegar

1 tablespoon ancho chile powder (see Note)

½ cup finely chopped cilantro

½ cup finely chopped flat-leaf parsley

¼ cup finely chopped oregano leaves

⅓ cup olive oil

Place all the ingredients in a food processor and process until smooth. Makes about 2½ cups.

FOR THE STEAKS:

8 rib-eye steaks (10 ounces each)

Chimichurri Marinade

Kosher salt and freshly ground pepper

Dried Chile–Mustard Sauce

Place the steaks in a large shallow baking dish or pan, cover with the marinade, and turn to coat. Refrigerate, covered, for 1 to 4 hours.

Preheat a gas or charcoal grill to high. Remove steaks from the marinade, shaking off any excess, and season with salt and pepper (discard the used marinade). Grill until golden brown on one side, 3 to 4 minutes. Turn over and continue cooking 3 to 4 minutes for medium rare.

Place the steaks on a platter and serve Dried Chile–Mustard Sauce alongside.

NOTE: Ancho chile powder is available at Hispanic or gourmet markets, or from Kitchen Market, 218 Eighth Avenue, New York, NY 10011, 212-243-4433, which has a mail-order list.

Pan-Seared Porterhouse Steaks with Honey-Mustard Pan Juice

MAKES 8 SERVINGS

Sure, you can cook a porterhouse directly on the grill, but you can't make the honey-mustard pan juice unless you use a pan, and the juice is awesome. After the steak has cooked in the hot pan, take it out and let it rest. Add the juice ingredients to the pan, scrape up all the delicious bits of meat that have caramelized on the bottom, and pour the delicious mixture over the steak. This recipe also works well on a stovetop.

Be sure to use a nonreactive pan, such as stainless steel or enamel-coated cast iron. Uncoated cast iron or aluminum pans can react with acids in food, causing changes in color or flavor.

FOR THE STEAKS:

¼ cup olive oil
4 porterhouse steaks (about 22 ounces each)
Kosher salt and freshly ground pepper

Preheat a gas or charcoal grill to medium high.

Season 2 steaks with salt and pepper. Heat 2 tablespoons of the oil until almost smoking in a large nonreactive skillet set on the grill and cook the seasoned steaks until golden brown on one side, 3 to 4 minutes. Turn over and continue cooking 4 to 5 minutes for medium rare. Remove to a rack on the grill away from the heat, and repeat with the remaining steaks.

(continued)

149

FOR THE HONEY-MUSTARD PAN JUICE:

2 shallots, finely chopped

1½ cups chicken stock, homemade or low-sodium canned

2 tablespoons fresh lemon juice

2 tablespoons Dijon mustard

1 tablespoon honey

¼ cup coarsely chopped fresh parsley

Kosher salt and freshly ground pepper

Pour all but 1 tablespoon of oil from the pan, add the shallots, and cook until soft, 2 to 3 minutes. Add the stock and lemon juice and cook, stirring and scraping up the bits of meat stuck to the bottom of the pan, until reduced to 1 cup. Whisk in the mustard and honey and cook for 2 minutes. Add the parsley and season with salt and pepper.

Place the steaks on a platter and drizzle with the sauce.

Black Pepper and Molasses–Glazed Filet Mignon

MAKES 8 SERVINGS

Filet mignon is always going to be very tender, but it needs an infusion of flavor. I take deep, rich molasses and cut it with a lot of cracked black pepper, then glaze the filet while it grills. I like to cook the glazed filet whole, then take it off the grill and slice it, so each piece has a crust. Cook carefully, so the glaze will caramelize, but not burn, and the flavors will cook into the steak.

150

FOR THE MOLASSES GLAZE:

   2 tablespoons olive oil
   1 small onion, finely chopped
   2 cloves garlic, finely chopped
   1 tablespoon finely grated gingerroot
   ¼ cup dark rum
   1 cup dark molasses
   3 cups freshly squeezed orange juice
   3 tablespoons cracked black pepper
   Kosher salt

Heat the oil in a small saucepan over medium-high heat until almost smoking, and cook the onion until soft, 4 to 5 minutes. Add the garlic and gingerroot and cook an additional 2 minutes. Add the rum and reduce until completely dry. Add the molasses, orange juice, and pepper, season with salt, and cook until reduced to 1 cup, 15 to 20 minutes. Let cool at room temperature. May be refrigerated, covered, for 1 day; use at room temperature. Makes about 1 cup.

FOR THE FILETS MIGNON:

   Two 2-pound pieces of beef filet
   Olive oil for brushing the meat
   Kosher salt
   Molasses Glaze

Preheat a gas or charcoal grill to medium.

Brush the meat with olive oil and season with salt. Grill until well seared on one side, 4 minutes, turn over, and baste with the Molasses Glaze. Continue grilling for 3 minutes, turn over, baste, and grill for 2 to 3 minutes more (a total of 10 minutes), for medium rare. Let rest for 10 minutes; then slice into 8 steaks.

151

GRILLED STEAK SALAD WITH POBLANO VINAIGRETTE

MAKES 8 SERVINGS

This one is for the healthy meat eaters: along with your protein, you're getting ripe tomatoes, crisp baby spinach, and sweet Vidalia onions. Grilling the meat with Mesa Steak Sauce gives it extra flavor and a beautiful glazed crust.

FOR THE MESA STEAK SAUCE:

2 cups ketchup

½ cup ground fresh horseradish, or prepared horseradish, drained

2 tablespoons honey

2 tablespoons Dijon mustard

2 tablespoons maple syrup

1 teaspoon Worcestershire sauce

2 tablespoons ancho chile powder (see Note)

Kosher salt and freshly ground white pepper

In a small bowl, mix the ketchup, horseradish, honey, mustard, maple syrup, Worcestershire sauce, and ancho chile powder until combined. Season with salt and pepper. May be refrigerated up to 1 week. Makes 2½ cups.

FOR THE POBLANO VINAIGRETTE:

2 poblano peppers
¾ cup olive oil, plus extra for rubbing the poblanos
¼ cup chopped red onion
¼ cup fresh lime juice
½ cup spinach leaves
1 teaspoon honey
Kosher salt and freshly ground pepper

Preheat a gas or charcoal grill to medium high.

Rub the poblanos with the olive oil and grill, turning, until charred on all sides, 3 to 5 minutes. Seed them and chop coarsely.

Combine the grilled poblanos, the remaining ¾ cup olive oil, the onion, lime juice, spinach , and honey in a blender and blend until smooth. Season with salt and pepper and pour into a squeeze bottle. May be refrigerated for 1 day; serve at room temperature. Makes about 1½ cups.

FOR THE STEAKS:

8 rib-eye steaks (8 to 10 ounces each)
2 cups Mesa Steak Sauce
Kosher salt and freshly ground pepper

Place the steaks in a shallow pan or baking dish and cover with the steak sauce. Refrigerate, covered, for 2 hours or overnight, turning once.

Preheat a gas or charcoal grill to high.

Remove the steaks from the marinade, shaking off any excess (discard the used marinade), and season with salt and pepper.

Grill until well seared, 3 to 4 minutes. Turn over and continue grilling 4 to 5 minutes for medium rare.

(continued)

153

BEEF, LAMB, PORK, AND RIBS

FOR THE SALAD:

Olive oil for brushing the onion and tomatoes,
   plus 3 tablespoons

1 large Vidalia onion, sliced ½ inch thick

8 plum tomatoes, halved

Kosher salt and freshly ground pepper

2 pounds baby spinach, washed well

3 tablespoons balsamic vinegar

Grilled steak

Poblano Vinaigrette

½ pound Cabrales blue cheese, crumbled

Brush the onion and tomatoes with olive oil and season with salt and pepper.

Grill on both sides until just cooked through. Place the spinach in a large bowl and toss with the balsamic vinegar, 3 tablespoons of olive oil, and salt and pepper to taste.

Cut the steaks into ½-inch-thick slices and arrange on top of the spinach. Garnish with the grilled tomatoes and onion, drizzle with the Poblano Vinaigrette, and sprinkle with the Cabrales blue cheese.

NOTE: Ancho chile powder is available at Hispanic or gourmet markets, or from Kitchen Market, 218 Eighth Avenue, New York, NY 10011, 212-243-4433, which has a mail-order list.

Moroccan Spice–Rubbed Leg of Lamb with Apricot Chutney

MAKES 8 SERVINGS

Sear this leg of lamb over a medium fire and then finish it on the rotisserie. The lamb will become crisp on the outside, as the inside cooks slowly to juicy perfection.

FOR THE APRICOT CHUTNEY:

> **2 cups dried unsulfured apricots**
> **2 tablespoons olive oil**
> **1 large yellow onion, finely chopped**
> **2 cloves garlic, finely chopped**
> **1 tablespoon peeled and finely chopped gingerroot**
> **1 jalapeño pepper, finely chopped**
> **2 tablespoons light brown sugar**
> **1 cup cider vinegar**
> **¼ cup coarsely chopped cilantro**
> **Kosher salt and freshly ground pepper**

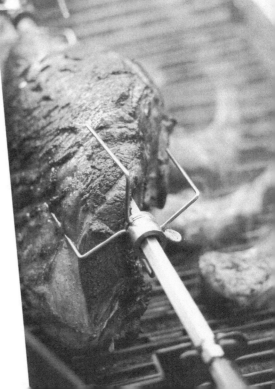

In a small bowl, soak the apricots in hot water to cover for 30 minutes; drain, and chop coarsely.

On a side burner (or the stove), heat the olive oil in a small saucepan over medium-high heat until almost smoking and cook the onion until soft and lightly golden, 6 to 7 minutes. Add the garlic, gingerroot, and jalapeño and cook for 2 minutes. Add the apricots, brown sugar, and vinegar, and bring to a boil. Reduce the heat to medium and simmer 30 minutes,

(continued)

155

stirring occasionally. Add the cilantro and season with salt and pepper. May be refrigerated, covered, up to 3 days; serve at room temperature. Makes 3 cups.

FOR THE SPICE RUB:

¼ cup Hungarian paprika

2 tablespoons light brown sugar

1 tablespoon ground cumin

1 tablespoon cinnamon

2 teaspoons ground coriander

4 cloves garlic, mashed to a paste

1 teaspoon kosher salt

1 teaspoon freshly ground black pepper

Mix all the ingredients together in a small bowl.

FOR THE LAMB:

1 boneless leg of lamb (7 pounds)

Olive oil for brushing the lamb

Spice rub

Preheat a gas or charcoal grill to medium.

Brush the lamb with olive oil and rub the spice rub into the meat on all sides. Grill until seared, 4 to 5 minutes on each side, and then place on a rotisserie. Cook, with the cover closed, until medium rare, 1¼ to 1½ hours. Let rest 10 to 15 minutes.

Slice thinly and place on a large platter. Serve the Apricot Chutney alongside.

Lamb and Red Onion Tacos with Tomato-Mint Relish

MAKES 8 SERVINGS

Leftover lamb from the night before makes a perfect lunch the next day, to take to the beach or on a picnic. Or grill the lamb especially for the tacos—they're worth it.

FOR THE TOMATO-MINT RELISH:

- 4 large tomatoes, coarsely chopped
- ¼ cup finely diced red onion
- 1 jalapeño pepper, seeded and minced
- 3 tablespoons balsamic vinegar
- ¼ cup fresh mint, chiffonade (see Note 1)
- 1 tablespoon olive oil
- Kosher salt and freshly ground pepper

Combine all the ingredients in a bowl and let sit for 1 hour at room temperature. May be refrigerated for 1 day; serve at room temperature. Makes about 2½ cups.

FOR THE LAMB MARINADE:

- 2 tablespoons ancho chile powder (see Note 2)
- 1 small onion, coarsely chopped
- 10 cloves garlic, coarsely chopped
- 2 chipotle peppers, coarsely chopped
- 1 cup fresh orange juice
- 1 cup olive oil

(continued)

In a blender, combine the ancho powder, onion, garlic, chipotle, and orange juice and blend until smooth. With the motor running, slowly add the olive oil and blend until emulsified. May be refrigerated for 1 day; use at room temperature. Makes about 2½ cups.

FOR THE LAMB:

2 lamb tenderloins (about 2 pounds each)
Lamb marinade
Kosher salt and freshly ground pepper

Place the lamb in a shallow pan or baking dish, cover with the lamb marinade, and refrigerate, covered, for 2 to 4 hours.

Preheat a gas or charcoal grill to high.

Remove the lamb from the marinade, shaking off the excess (discard the used marinade). Season the lamb with salt and pepper and grill until medium rare, 4 to 5 minutes on each side. Let sit 10 minutes, then cut into thin slices.

TO ASSEMBLE THE TACOS:

8 flour tortillas
1 cup grated Monterey Jack cheese
1 cup grated white Cheddar cheese
½ cup crumbled feta cheese
1 large red onion, sliced thin and grilled
¼ cup fresh mint, chiffonade (see Note 1)
Kosher salt and freshly ground pepper
Olive oil for brushing the tacos

For each taco: Place four slices of lamb over half the tortilla. Sprinkle with 2 tablespoons each of the Jack and Cheddar cheeses and 1 tablespoon of the feta cheese. Top with one-eighth of the grilled onion and the mint. Season with salt and pepper. Fold over the tortilla and brush the top with olive oil.

Grill oiled-side down until crisp, about 3 minutes. Brush the top with oil, turn over the taco, and grill until crisp and the cheese has melted, about another 3 minutes.

Place on a large platter and cut into halves. Serve the Tomato-Mint Relish on the side.

NOTES:

1. To cut mint into chiffonade, or fine ribbons, roll up the leaves and cut into thin strips.

2. Ancho chile powder is available at Hispanic or gourmet markets, or from Kitchen Market, 218 Eighth Avenue, New York, NY 10011, 212-243-4433, which has a mail-order list.

Tarragon-Marinated Lamb Chops with Pineapple-Pecan Relish

The sweet, anise notes of tarragon make this a beautiful dinner party dish, slightly more formal than my usual style—call it candlelight grilling. Grilled pineapple, chopped pecans, and some more fresh tarragon combine in the accompanying relish.

FOR THE PINEAPPLE-PECAN RELISH:

- 1 medium pineapple, peeled, cored, and cut into ½-inch dice
- 1 small red onion, finely diced
- 3 tablespoons balsamic vinegar
- 3 tablespoons olive oil
- 2 tablespoons finely chopped tarragon
- 2 tablespoons finely chopped flat-leaf parsley
- Kosher salt and freshly ground pepper
- ½ cup coarsely chopped toasted pecans

Combine the pineapple, onion, vinegar, olive oil, and herbs in a medium bowl and season with salt and pepper. Just before serving, fold in the pecans. May be refrigerated, covered (without the pecans) for 1 day; serve at room temperature. Makes 2 to 2½ cups.

FOR THE TARRAGON-MARINATED LAMB CHOPS:

½ cup olive oil
¼ cup coarsely chopped fresh tarragon
4 cloves garlic
32 baby lamb chops (each 2 ounces and ¾ inch thick)
Kosher salt and freshly ground pepper

Combine the olive oil, tarragon, and garlic in a large shallow baking dish, add the lamb chops, and turn to coat well. Refrigerate, covered, 2 to 4 hours.

Preheat a gas or charcoal grill to medium high.

Remove the chops from the marinade, shaking off the excess (discard the used marinade). Season the chops on both sides with salt and pepper and grill until medium, 3 to 4 minutes on each side.

Place on a serving platter and serve the Pineapple-Pecan Relish alongside.

Lamb Chops with Habañero-Mint Glaze

MAKES 8 SERVINGS

Lamb chops with mint remind me of my childhood, except my mom didn't use habañero chiles at that time. It's fun to rethink classic combinations, though, and to slip in a surprise.

FOR THE HABAÑERO-MINT GLAZE:

3 cups red wine vinegar

3 cups sugar

2 habañero peppers, coarsely chopped

½ cup fresh mint, chiffonade (fine ribbons)

Kosher salt and freshly ground pepper

Combine the vinegar, sugar, and habañeros in a nonreactive medium saucepan and bring to a boil over high heat. Cook until reduced to a thick syrup, about 20 minutes. Remove from the heat and mix in the mint, season with salt and pepper, and let cool to room temperature. May be refrigerated up to 3 days; use at room temperature. Makes 1¼ cups.

FOR THE LAMB CHOPS:

Eight 2-inch-thick loin lamb chops (8 ounces each), trimmed

Olive oil for brushing the chops

Kosher salt and freshly ground pepper

Habañero-Mint Glaze

Preheat a gas or charcoal grill to medium high.

Brush the lamb chops on both sides with olive oil and season with salt and pepper. Grill until medium rare, 3 to 4 minutes on each side. During the last 2 minutes of grilling time, brush the chops on both sides with the Habañero-Mint Glaze.

Place on a large serving platter and brush again with the glaze.

Lamb Chops with Mustard-Molasses Glaze

MAKES 8 SERVINGS

Hot mustard and sweet molasses play off the lamb, which drinks up big flavors like these. The glaze couldn't be simpler to put together.

FOR THE MUSTARD-MOLASSES GLAZE:

> 1 cup dark molasses
>
> 3 tablespoons Dijon mustard
>
> 2 tablespoons balsamic vinegar
>
> 1 tablespoon ancho chile powder (see Note)
>
> 2 cloves garlic, finely chopped

In a small bowl, mix all the ingredients together until combined.

FOR THE LAMB CHOPS:

> 8 loin or rib lamb chops (each 8 ounces and ¾ inch thick)
>
> Olive oil for brushing the chops
>
> Kosher salt and freshly ground pepper
>
> Molasses-Mustard Glaze

Preheat a gas or charcoal grill to medium.

Brush each lamb chop on both sides with olive oil and season with salt and pepper. Cook until golden brown, 3 to 4 minutes. Turn over and cook an additional 3 to 4 minutes for medium rare. During the last 2 minutes of cooking, brush the chops on both sides with the Molasses-Mustard Glaze.

NOTE: Ancho chile powder is available at Hispanic or gourmet markets, or mail order from Kitchen Market, 218 Eighth Avenue, New York, NY 10011, 212-243-4433.

163

LOIN OF LAMB RUBBED WITH GARLIC AND CUMIN WITH GRILLED LEMONS, YOGURT SAUCE, AND GRILLED PITA

MAKES 8 SERVINGS

In Greece, I tasted lamb infused with the flavors of garlic, cumin, lemon, and yogurt—an amazing combination. Tender loin of lamb works best for this dish, cooked quickly, so the garlic doesn't burn. Serve with grilled lemon halves (another Greek note) and plenty of grilled pita bread.

FOR THE YOGURT SAUCE:

2 cups plain yogurt, drained (see Note)
2 ripe plum tomatoes, seeded and finely chopped
2 cloves garlic, minced
¼ cup finely chopped cilantro
1 tablespoon lime juice
Kosher salt and finely ground pepper

Combine the drained yogurt, tomatoes, garlic, cilantro, and lime juice in a medium bowl and season with salt and pepper. Let sit at room temperature for half an hour before serving, to blend the flavors. May be refrigerated for 1 day; serve at room temperature. Makes about 2 cups.

FOR THE GRILLED LEMONS:

8 lemons, halved
Olive oil for brushing
Kosher salt and freshly ground pepper

164

Preheat a gas or charcoal grill to high.

Brush the lemons with olive oil and season with salt and pepper. Grill cut-side down on the preheated grill until marked, about 2 minutes. Turn over and grill another 2 minutes.

FOR THE LOIN OF LAMB:

¼ cup olive oil
2 tablespoons ground cumin
8 cloves garlic, smashed
2 tablespoons fresh lime juice
2 tablespoons coarsely chopped cilantro
¼ teaspoon coarsely ground black pepper
2 loins of lamb (2 pounds each)
Kosher salt

Place the oil, cumin, garlic, lime juice, cilantro, and pepper in a food processor and process to a smooth paste. Place the lamb in a large shallow baking dish or pan and rub the lamb completely with the olive oil and garlic mixture. Refrigerate, covered, for 1 to 4 hours.

Preheat a gas or charcoal grill to high.

Remove the meat from the marinade, shaking off the excess (discard the used marinade), and season with salt and pepper.

Place the lamb on the grill just until seared on each side. (The lemons also may be grilled now.) Turn down the heat to medium on a gas grill, or move the lamb to a cooler part of a charcoal grill, and finish cooking to medium rare. The total time should be 4 to 5 minutes on each side. Let rest 10 minutes.

FOR THE GRILLED PITA:

8 pocketless pita breads
Olive oil for brushing

(continued)

165

Brush the pita with oil on both sides and place on the preheated medium grill until golden brown, 30 to 45 seconds on each side.

To serve, slice the lamb thinly on the bias and arrange on a serving platter, surrounded by the lemons and pita bread. Serve the Yogurt Sauce alongside.

NOTE: To drain yogurt, place it in a cheesecloth-lined strainer over a bowl for 1 hour, until thickened. Discard the liquid that remains in the bowl.

Pork Chops with Horseradish-Maple Glaze

MAKES 8 SERVINGS

Think about these three flavors going together—grilled pork chops, pungent horseradish, and sweet maple syrup—it makes sense. We've been doing this popular dish at Mesa Grill for a long time.

FOR THE HORSERADISH-MAPLE GLAZE:

1½ cups maple syrup

¼ cup grated fresh horseradish,
  or prepared horseradish, drained

1 tablespoon Dijon mustard

1 tablespoon ancho chile powder (see Note)

Combine all the ingredients in a medium bowl. May be refrigerated, covered, for 1 day; use at room temperature. Makes about 1¾ cups.

FOR THE PORK CHOPS:

8 pork chops (each 6 ounces and 1 inch thick)
Olive oil for brushing the chops
Kosher salt and freshly ground pepper
Horseradish-Maple Glaze

Preheat a gas or charcoal grill to medium high.

Reserve ¾ cup of glaze and use the remainder for brushing during cooking. Brush the chops on both sides with olive oil and season with salt and pepper. Grill for 3 to 4 minutes, brush with glaze, and turn over. Grill for another 3 to 4 minutes, brush, and turn again, for medium-well doneness.

Arrange the chops on a serving platter and brush with the reserved ¾ cup of glaze.

NOTE: Ancho chile powder is available at Hispanic or gourmet markets, or from Kitchen Market, 218 Eighth Avenue, New York, NY 10011, 212-243-4433, which has a mail-order list.

167

Hoisin-Marinated Pork Chops with Pineapple–Green Onion Relish

MAKES 8 SERVINGS

I like to cut these pork chops thin, the way they are cut in Asian restaurants, the better to absorb the hoisin sauce, a Chinese condiment with sweet-tart flavor and hints of garlic and chile. Pineapple and scallions are opposites in flavor, but they combine to make sense in this summer relish.

FOR THE PINEAPPLE–GREEN ONION RELISH:

- 6 green onions (white bulbs and 3 inches of green)
- 2 tablespoons olive oil, plus extra for brushing the green onions
- Kosher salt and freshly ground pepper
- 1 medium ripe pineapple, peeled and diced
- 1 jalapeño pepper, finely chopped
- 2 tablespoons fresh lime juice
- 1 tablespoon honey
- 2 tablespoons coarsely chopped cilantro

Preheat a gas or charcoal grill to high.

Brush the green onions with olive oil and season with salt and pepper. Grill until almost cooked through, 4 to 5 minutes, and finely slice. Place in a medium bowl and add the pineapple, jalapeño, lime juice, honey, cilantro, and the remaining 2 tablespoons of olive oil, and stir to combine. May be refrigerated for 1 day; serve at room temperature. Makes about 4 cups.

FOR THE PORK CHOPS:

- 1 cup hoisin sauce
- 3 tablespoons rice wine vinegar
- 2 tablespoons soy sauce
- 4 cloves garlic, coarsely chopped
- 1 teaspoon sesame oil
- 16 thin pork chops cut from the loin (about 4 ounces each)
- Kosher salt and freshly ground pepper
- Pineapple–Green Onion Relish

In a small bowl, combine the hoisin sauce, vinegar, soy sauce, garlic, and sesame oil. Place the chops in a shallow pan or baking dish, pour the marinade over them, and refrigerate, covered, 2 to 3 hours, turning once.

Preheat a gas or charcoal grill to high.

Remove the chops from the marinade, shaking off the excess (discard the used marinade). Season with salt and pepper and grill 2 to 3 minutes on each side for medium well.

Arrange on a large serving platter. Serve the Pineapple–Green Onion Relish alongside.

169

Pork Chops Marinated in Orange, Ginger, and Toasted Paprika

MAKES 8 SERVINGS

When you toast paprika in a pan it takes on a sort of nutty flavor that is fabulous. You can even put the pan on the grill, instead of a stovetop, and do the whole thing outside. These pork chops get a lot of flavor from a long soak in orange juice and fresh ginger, which makes them the exception to my rule about brief marinades.

FOR THE ORANGE, GINGER, AND TOASTED PAPRIKA MARINADE:

- 2 tablespoons olive oil
- 1 small onion, finely chopped
- 4 cloves garlic, finely chopped
- 2 tablespoons Spanish paprika
- 6 cups fresh orange juice
- 2 tablespoons peeled and coarsely chopped gingerroot

In a medium saucepan over medium-high heat, heat the oil until almost smoking and cook the onion and garlic until soft. Add the paprika and cook until lightly toasted and fragrant, about 2 minutes. Raise the heat to high, add the orange juice and gingerroot, and bring to a boil. Continue cooking, stirring occasionally, until the orange juice has reduced to 2 cups. Remove the marinade from the heat and let it cool completely at room temperature. May be refrigerated for 1 day; use at room temperature. Makes about 2½ cups.

FOR THE PORK CHOPS:

8 thick-cut pork chops (6 ounces each)
Kosher salt and freshly ground pepper
Orange, Ginger, and Toasted Paprika Marinade

Place the pork chops in a large, shallow pan or baking dish and cover with 2 cups of the Orange, Ginger, and Toasted Paprika Marinade, turning the chops to coat completely (reserve the remaining ½ cup marinade). Refrigerate, covered, 2 to 4 hours.

Preheat a gas or charcoal grill to high. Remove the chops from the marinade and shake off any excess (discard the used marinade). Grill until golden brown, 4 to 5 minutes; then turn and continue grilling until cooked through, 3 to 4 minutes more.

Arrange on a serving platter and brush with the reserved marinade.

171

Grilled Pork Loin Sandwiches with Spicy Mango Ketchup

MAKES 8 SERVINGS

The sweet and spicy flavors of Mango Ketchup are a delicious foil for the savory grilled pork loin, as are the strips of smoky grilled bell peppers. This is a satisfying lunchtime sandwich.

FOR THE PORK LOINS:

2 boneless pork loins (2 pounds each), sliced ¼ inch thick

Vegetable oil for brushing the pork loins

Kosher salt and freshly ground pepper

Preheat a gas or charcoal grill to high. Brush the pork loin slices with oil and season with salt and pepper. Grill until marked and cooked through, about 2 minutes on each side.

TO ASSEMBLE:

8 Kaiser rolls, split

Mango Ketchup (page 20)

2 medium red bell peppers, grilled and julienned (see Note)

2 medium yellow bell peppers, grilled and julienned (see Note)

Grill the rolls split-side down until toasted, about 30 seconds. Divide the sliced pork loin among the split rolls and top with red and yellow grilled pepper strips and a dollop of Mango Ketchup.

NOTE: To grill the bell peppers, brush with olive oil and season with salt and pepper. Grill over high heat until charred on all sides. Let sit in a bowl, covered with plastic wrap, for 15 minutes. Peel, halve, and seed. To julienne, cut into small matchsticks.

172

Grilled Mozzarella and Black Pepper Quesadilla with Prosciutto di Parma

MAKES 8 SERVINGS

This dish reminds me of a white pizza I love to order at Italian restaurants. I put fresh mozzarella in a tortilla, top it with sweet red onion and freshly ground black pepper, and grill it until the mozzarella melts and the tortilla is golden and smoky. I top it with thin slices of savory prosciutto, for delicious contrast with the mellow cheese. The sharp herbal flavor of rosemary oil heightens all the other flavors.

FOR THE ROSEMARY OIL:

- 1 cup olive oil
- ¼ cup rosemary leaves
- ¼ cup coarsely chopped chives
- Kosher salt and freshly ground pepper

In a food processor, combine the oil, rosemary, chives, salt, and pepper and process until smooth. Strain and refrigerate. May be refrigerated for 1 day; serve at room temperature.

(continued)

FOR THE QUESADILLAS:

Twelve 6-inch flour tortillas (or cut 8-inch tortillas to size, using a 6-inch plate as a guide)

¾ pound fresh mozzarella, thinly sliced

1 red onion, thinly sliced

2 tablespoons cracked black pepper

16 thin slices prosciutto

Rosemary Oil

Preheat a gas or charcoal grill to high.

Place 4 tortillas on a work surface and top each with some of the mozzarella and a slice or two of onion, sprinkle with salt, and season generously with black pepper. Cover with another tortilla layer and repeat. Top with a final layer of tortillas and brush with oil. Grill oiled-side down until golden brown, 2 to 3 minutes. Brush with oil, turn, and grill until the other side is golden brown and the cheese has melted, another 2 to 3 minutes.

Place on a serving platter and cut into quarters. Top each quarter with a slice of prosciutto and drizzle with Rosemary Oil.

Spicy Barbecued Ribs with Peanut–Green Onion Relish

MAKES 8 SERVINGS

These ribs are a winner at Mesa Grill—if I take them off the menu for even a day, people line up and complain to me. As the ribs cook, they become crusted with a sweet, dark, russet-colored bark, and when they are done, the tender meat just falls off the bones. A peanut-and-green-onion relish adds textural and taste contrasts.

FOR THE MARINADE:

- **2 cups soy sauce**
- **3 cups water**
- **¼ cup peeled and coarsely chopped gingerroot**
- **6 cloves garlic, coarsely chopped**
- **4 racks pork ribs (3 pounds each)**

Combine the soy sauce, water, gingerroot, and garlic in a medium saucepan over high heat and bring to a boil. Turn off the heat and let cool to room temperature. Place the ribs in a large roasting pan, cover with the marinade, and refrigerate, covered,
24 hours, no longer.

(continued)

175

FOR THE SPICY SAUCE:

2 tablespoons unsalted butter

1 large onion, finely diced

2 cloves garlic, finely diced

8 ripe plum tomatoes, coarsely chopped
   (or substitute canned tomatoes)

¼ cup ketchup

½ cup water

2 tablespoons Dijon mustard

2 tablespoons dark brown sugar

2 tablespoons honey

1 teaspoon cayenne

1 tablespoon ancho chile powder (see Note)

1 tablespoon paprika

1 tablespoon Worcestershire sauce

½ cup smooth peanut butter

¼ cup soy sauce

1 tablespoon rice wine vinegar

1 tablespoon canned chipotles, pureed (see Note)

In a large saucepan over medium-high heat, melt the butter and sweat the onion and garlic until translucent, about 5 minutes. Add the tomatoes, ketchup, and water and simmer 15 minutes. Add the mustard, sugar, honey, cayenne, ancho powder, paprika, and Worcestershire sauce and simmer another 20 minutes.

Pour the mixture into a food processor and process until smooth. Pour into a large bowl and whisk in the peanut butter, soy sauce, vinegar, and chipotle puree.

May be refrigerated, covered, for 2 days; use at room temperature. Makes about 3½ cups.

FOR THE PEANUT–GREEN ONION RELISH:

2 cups coarsely chopped roasted peanuts

**¼ cup finely sliced green onion
(white bulbs and 3 inches of green)**

¼ teaspoon cinnamon

1 teaspoon peeled finely grated gingerroot

½ teaspoon sugar

Combine all the ingredients in a medium bowl and serve immediately. (Ingredients may be prepared ahead and combined at the last minute.) Makes about 2¼ cups.

FOR THE RIBS:

The marinated ribs

Kosher salt and freshly ground pepper

Spicy Sauce

Peanut–Green Onion Relish

Preheat a gas grill to medium low. If using a charcoal grill, fill the entire grill with a shallow layer of charcoal and light the left outer edge only. As the fire moves from left to right, you will have consecutive areas of medium-low heat.

Season the ribs on both sides with salt and pepper. Grill slowly, with the cover closed, until tender, turning every 10 minutes, for 2 to 2½ hours. During the last 15 minutes of grilling, baste with some of the sauce. Remove from the grill and immediately brush with more of the sauce. Cut into single ribs and place on a large platter.

The ribs may be grilled up to 1 day ahead and refrigerated. Before serving, place on the grill until heated through. Serve with the Peanut–Green Onion Relish.

NOTE: Ancho chile powder and canned chipotle peppers in adobo are available at Hispanic or gourmet markets, or from Kitchen Market, 218 Eighth Avenue, New York, NY 10011, 212-243-4433, which has a mail-order list.

To make chipotle puree, process canned chipotles in a blender or food processor along with a little of their liquid.

177

Slow-Grilled Pork Ribs Basted with Dried Apricot and Fresh Mint Barbecue Glaze

MAKES 8 SERVINGS

Baste the ribs with this fruit- and herb-flavored sauce near the end of the grilling time, until it forms a caramelized crust. The apricot and mint flavors will become part of the meat.

FOR THE DRIED APRICOT AND FRESH MINT BARBECUE GLAZE:

2 tablespoons olive oil

1 large yellow onion, finely chopped

2 cloves garlic, coarsely chopped

2 tablespoons ancho chile powder (see Note 1)

4 cups red wine

4 cups red wine vinegar

2 cups sugar

6 dried unsulfured apricots, coarsely chopped

2 tablespoons tamarind pulp (see Note 1)

¼ cup mint, chiffonade (see Note 2)

Kosher salt and freshly ground pepper

Preheat a gas or charcoal grill to medium, or use a side burner (or the stove).

Heat the olive oil until almost smoking in a large saucepan and cook the onion until soft, 4 to 5 minutes. Add the garlic and ancho powder and cook for 2 minutes. Add the wine, vinegar, and sugar, increase the heat to high, and bring to a boil. Cook, stirring, until the sugar has dissolved, and continue cooking until reduced by half.

Add the apricots and cook until softened, about 15 minutes. Remove from the heat and add the tamarind pulp and mint.

Place the mixture in a food processor and process until smooth. Strain into a bowl and season with salt and pepper. Let cool to room temperature. May be refrigerated, covered, up to 3 days; use at room temperature. Makes 2 to 3 cups.

FOR THE RIBS:

4 racks pork ribs (3 pounds each)
Olive oil for brushing the ribs
Kosher salt and freshly ground pepper
Dried Apricot and Fresh Mint Barbecue Glaze

Preheat a gas grill to medium low. If using a charcoal grill, fill the entire grill with a shallow layer of charcoal and light the left outer edge only. As the fire moves from left to right, you will have consecutive areas of medium-low heat.

Brush the ribs on both sides with the olive oil, season with salt and pepper, and grill, with the cover closed, until tender, 2 to 2½ hours. During the last 30 minutes of grilling, baste on both sides with the Dried Apricot and Fresh Mint Barbecue Glaze every 15 minutes, until done. Remove from the grill and, if serving immediately, brush with more of the glaze, cut into single ribs, and place on a large platter.

The ribs may be grilled up to 1 day ahead and refrigerated, in which case do not brush them again as they come off the grill. Before serving, place on the grill until heated through. Remove from the grill, brush immediately with glaze, cut into single ribs, and place on a large platter.

NOTES:

1. Ancho chile powder and tamarind pulp are available at Hispanic or gourmet markets, or from Kitchen Market, 218 Eighth Avenue, New York, NY 10011, 212-243-4433, which has a mail-order list.

2. To cut mint into chiffonade, or fine ribbons, roll up the leaves and cut into thin strips.

179

INDIAN-SPICED BARBECUED RIBS

MAKES 8 SERVINGS

Indian spices can give a different twist to your traditional barbecue sauce, bringing in the flavors of coriander, cumin, ginger, and tamarind. This is a somewhat exotic version of the familiar barbecued ribs.

FOR THE INDIAN-SPICED BARBECUE SAUCE:

2 tablespoons olive oil
1 Spanish onion, coarsely chopped
6 cloves garlic, coarsely chopped
1 tablespoon peeled and grated gingerroot
1 tablespoon ground cumin
1 tablespoon ground coriander
1 teaspoon ground cinnamon
1/8 teaspoon ground cloves
1/4 teaspoon ground nutmeg
1 medium can plum tomatoes with their juice
   (about 2 cups)
1/2 cup light brown sugar
3 tablespoons tamarind concentrate or paste (see Note)
1 jalapeño pepper, coarsely chopped
1/4 cup coarsely chopped cilantro
Kosher salt and freshly ground pepper

Heat the olive oil until almost smoking in a large saucepan over medium-high heat, and cook the onion and garlic until soft, 4 to 5 minutes. Add the gingerroot and cook 2 minutes. Add the spices and cook until the flavors have mellowed, an additional 20 minutes. Add the tomatoes and their juice, the brown sugar, tamarind paste, and jalapeño, and stir to combine. Cook until thickened, 30 to 40 minutes, stirring occasionally.

Remove from the heat and add the cilantro. Place in a food processor and process until smooth. Season with salt and pepper. May be refrigerated, covered, up to 3 days; use at room temperature. Makes about 4 cups.

FOR THE RIBS:

4 racks pork ribs (3 pounds each)
Olive oil for brushing the ribs
Kosher salt and freshly ground pepper
Indian-Spiced Barbecue Sauce

Preheat a gas grill heat to medium low. If using a charcoal grill, fill the entire grill with a shallow layer of charcoal and light the left outer edge only. As the fire moves from left to right, you will have consecutive areas of medium-low heat.

Brush the ribs on both sides with olive oil and season on both sides with salt and pepper. Grill with the cover closed until tender, 2 to 2½ hours. During the last 15 minutes of grilling, baste with some of the Indian-Spiced Barbecue Sauce. Remove from the grill and, if serving immediately, brush with more of the sauce, cut into single ribs, and place on a large platter.

The ribs may be grilled up to 1 day ahead and refrigerated, in which case do not brush them again as they come off the grill. Before serving, place on the grill until heated through. Remove from the grill, brush immediately with sauce, cut into single ribs, and place on a large platter.

NOTE: Tamarind concentrate or paste is available at Hispanic or gourmet markets, or from Kitchen Market, 218 Eighth Avenue, New York, NY 10011, 212-243-4433, which has a mail-order list.

181

BEEF, LAMB, PORK, AND RIBS

6. VEGETABLES

Through the summer and fall, I wear a path from the farmers' market to my grill. Vegetables at the height of their season—sweet summer squash, golden corn, plump eggplant, and tomatoes bursting with juice—are irresistible cooked with just a brushing of olive oil and some fresh herbs or garlic. And vegetables that know no season—think mushrooms, onions, and potatoes—are great too. You can do a whole meal of vegetables, as I often do, or keep them as sparkling side dishes.

Fresh vegetables go quickly and simply from the grill to the table, and you don't have to be limited by traditional presentation. Grilled eggplant can become the centerpiece of some of the best salads, joining feta cheese; goat cheese, tomato, and basil; or crisp bell pepper. Similarly, salads can showcase grilled vegetables like corn, sweet or red onions, radicchio, and cherry tomatoes. Vegetables from asparagus to tomatoes blend with ease into risottos or soups, giving them entirely new flavors. Zucchini combines with goat cheese in crisp tortas, and classic ratatouille benefits from the smoky char of the grill. Add to these delicious potato salads that require no grilling at all, but make a hearty accent to any hot dishes. Or just grill some sweet, candylike Vidalia onions, add a salad or some flatbread, and you have a feast.

Vegetables have become more than just an important part of grilling—they've almost taken over. It's easy to make a complete meal out of any vegetable dish in this chapter; for example, Grilled Yellow Tomato–Yellow Pepper Soup with Torn Corn Tortillas; Eggplant "Sandwiches" with Goat Cheese, Tomato, and Basil; and Grilled Mushroom Tacos with White Truffle Oil. Or combine Grilled Asparagus Risotto with White Truffle Oil; Grilled Corn and Sweet Onion Salad; and Wild Mushrooms with Crushed Hazelnuts and Garlic. The farmers' market may easily be the only food store you need for several meals.

Most vegetables cook perfectly on the grill and come out with beautiful golden marks and tender texture, but you have to be smart about these things. Instead of just grillling for the sake of grilling (or for acclaim), you want to make sure it's going to work. If blanching something ahead of time and finishing it on the grill gives better results, that's what you should do, whether you're cooking corn, asparagus, or potatoes. Dense vegetables that take a long time should be blanched ahead, but so should some things that just need that preliminary softening. You are the best judge of your own vegetables.

RECIPES

Grilled Eggplant and Feta Cheese Salad

Grilled Eggplant and Pepper Salad
     with Cumin-Dusted Tortilla Chips

Eggplant "Sandwiches" with Goat
     Cheese, Tomato, and Basil

Grilled Zucchini and Goat Cheese
     Tortas with Spicy Hummus

Grilled Ratatouille

Asparagus with Parmesan Cheese
     and Prosciutto

Grilled Asparagus Risotto
     with White Truffle Oil

Grilled Yellow Tomato–Yellow Pepper
     Soup with Torn Corn Tortillas

Charred Corn Polenta with
     Grilled Tomato Vinaigrette

Grilled Corn and Sweet Onion Salad

Corn Niblets with Lime Butter
     and Tarragon

Corn on the Cob with Red Chile–Green
     Onion Butter

Grilled Radicchio and Goat Cheese
     Salad with a Balsamic-Honey Glaze

Grilled Red Onion and Cucumber Salad
     with Yogurt-Mint Dressing

Grilled Sweet Onion and Tomato Salad

Grilled Cherry Tomato and Watercress
     Salad with Green Garlic Vinaigrette

Napa Cabbage and Sesame Seed Slaw

Wild Mushrooms with Crushed
     Hazelnuts and Garlic

Grilled Mushroom Tacos with
     White Truffle Oil

Grilled Mushroom and Potato Salad
     with Dijon Mustard Dressing

Toasted Israeli Couscous Salad with
     Grilled Summer Vegetables

New Potato and Smoked Salmon Salad
     with Mustard–Fresh Dill Dressing

Warm Potato and Sweet Onion Salad
     with Bacon Dressing

Mesa Grill Potato Salad

Grilled Sweet Potato
     and Green Onion Salad

Spicy Hummus Dip with Grilled Pita
     and Vegetables

Prosciutto-Wrapped Grilled Figs with
     Smoked Mozzarella and Rosemary Oil

Grilled Crudités with
     Cabrales Blue Cheese

GRILLED EGGPLANT AND FETA CHEESE SALAD

MAKES 8 SERVINGS

The Greek influence on this dish is deliciously obvious. Smoky grilled eggplant, briny feta cheese, and fresh herbs are all you need. Mix them up with oil and vinegar and some salt and pepper, and you have a great salad.

1 eggplant (about 1 pound), cut into ½-inch slices

¼ cup olive oil, plus extra for brushing the eggplant

Kosher salt and freshly ground pepper

4 cloves garlic, minced

2 teaspoons ancho chile powder (see Note)

2 teaspoons finely chopped fresh oregano

3 tablespoons red wine vinegar

1 red onion, thinly sliced

8 ounces feta cheese, crumbled

Preheat a gas or charcoal grill to high.

Brush the eggplant with olive oil, season with salt and pepper, and grill until soft, with visible grill marks, about 4 minutes on each side. Cut into 4-inch cubes.

Whisk together the remaining ¼ cup of olive oil, garlic, chile powder, oregano, and vinegar in a large bowl until combined. Add the eggplant and red onion, toss to coat with dressing, season with salt and pepper, and crumble the feta cheese over the top.

NOTE: Ancho chile powder is available at Hispanic or gourmet markets, or from Kitchen Market, 218 Eighth Avenue, New York, NY 10011, 212-243-4433, which has a mail-order list.

185

Grilled Eggplant and Pepper Salad with Cumin-Dusted Tortilla Chips

MAKES 8 SERVINGS

This eggplant salad gives a good start to an outdoor party and with the spicy cumin chips, it goes well with all kinds of frosty drinks. Eggplant can take a lot of flavor, so I put in fresh garlic and oregano, along with some crumbled goat cheese, for a contrasting texture.

FOR THE CUMIN-DUSTED TORTILLA CHIPS:

- 6 cups peanut oil
- Ten 8-inch flour tortillas, cut into 8 wedges
- 3 tablespoons ground cumin
- 2 tablespoons kosher salt

Heat the oil in a large saucepan over high heat to 365°F, or until a piece of tortilla sizzles when immersed. Fry the tortilla wedges in batches until crisp, about 2 minutes per batch, and drain on paper towels. Combine the cumin and salt and season the tortillas with the mixture while still warm.

FOR THE GRILLED EGGPLANT AND PEPPER SALAD:

3 Asian eggplants, cut lengthwise ½ inch thick

2 large red bell peppers, quartered and seeded

2 large yellow bell peppers, quartered and seeded

1 medium red onion, peeled and quartered

2 tablespoons olive oil plus extra for brushing the eggplants,
    bell peppers, and onion

Kosher salt and freshly ground pepper

3 cloves garlic, finely chopped

2 tablespoons lemon juice

4 ounces soft goat cheese, crumbled

2 tablespoons finely chopped oregano

Cumin-Dusted Tortilla Chips

Preheat a gas or charcoal grill to medium high.

Brush the eggplants, bell peppers, and onion on both sides with some olive oil and season with salt and pepper. Grill until lightly golden brown and almost cooked through, 3 to 4 minutes on each side.

Cut into ½-inch dice and place in a medium bowl. Add the garlic, lemon juice, goat cheese, 2 tablespoons olive oil, and oregano and combine well. May be refrigerated for 1 day; serve at room temperature.

Place the salad in a large bowl and serve with the Cumin-Dusted Tortilla Chips.

187

Eggplant "Sandwiches" with Goat Cheese, Tomato, and Basil

MAKES 8 SERVINGS

For this breadless sandwich, grill marinated slices of eggplant and tomato and stack them in layers with goat cheese and basil. Then grill the savory sandwiches and serve them drizzled with fragrant basil oil.

FOR THE BASIL OIL:

1 cup olive oil
1 cup packed basil leaves
Kosher salt and freshly ground pepper

Combine the olive oil and basil leaves in a food processor and season with salt and pepper. Process until pureed (there will be some sediment), about 5 minutes. Strain into a squeeze bottle. May be refrigerated for 1 day; use at room temperature. Makes about 1¼ cup.

188

FOR THE EGGPLANT SANDWICHES:

2 medium eggplants (about 1 pound each),
  cut crosswise into ¼-inch slices (16 slices)

2 large beefsteak tomatoes, cut into ¼-inch slices
  (8 slices)

1½ cups olive oil

2 tablespoons balsamic vinegar

6 cloves garlic, coarsely chopped

8 ounces goat cheese, thinly sliced

½ cup packed basil leaves, chiffonade (see Note)

Kosher salt and freshly ground pepper

Basil Oil

Combine the olive oil, balsamic vinegar, and garlic and divide between two large bowls. Add the eggplant to one bowl and the tomatoes to the other and let marinate 1 hour, refrigerated.

Preheat a gas or charcoal grill to high.

Remove the eggplant and tomatoes from the marinade, shaking off any excess, and season with salt and pepper on both sides. (Discard the used marinade.) Grill the eggplant until golden brown and cooked through, about 3 minutes on each side; grill the tomatoes just until marked.

Place 8 slices of eggplant on a work surface and top each with a slice of tomato. Place a slice of goat cheese over the tomato and sprinkle with the basil (some basil will be left over). Cover with the remaining eggplant slices. Place the sandwiches on the grill just until the cheese has softened, about 1 minute, turning once.

Arrange the eggplant sandwiches on a platter and drizzle with the Basil Oil.

NOTE: To cut basil into chiffonade, or fine ribbons, roll up the leaves and cut into thin strips.

GRILLED ZUCCHINI AND GOAT CHEESE TORTAS WITH SPICY HUMMUS

MAKES 8 SERVINGS

These tortas are like little zucchini cakes, bound with tortillas. Cook them with the cover closed, so the grill acts as an oven. Tahini, an essential ingredient in hummus, is a smooth butter made from sesame seeds that is easy to find in most supermarkets.

FOR THE SPICY HUMMUS:

 1½ cups cooked or canned chick-peas, drained and rinsed
 3 cloves roasted garlic (see Note 1)
 1 chipotle pepper, canned in adobo (see Note 2)
 1 teaspoon ground cumin
 2 teaspoons honey
 2 tablespoons fresh lemon juice
 2 tablespoons tahini
 ¼ cup olive oil
 1½ tablespoons coarsely chopped flat-leaf parsley
 Kosher salt and freshly ground pepper

Place the chick-peas, garlic, chipotle, cumin, honey, lemon juice, and tahini in a food processor and process until smooth. With the motor running, slowly add the olive oil until emulsified. Add the parsley and season with salt and pepper. May be refrigerated for 1 day; serve at room temperature. Makes about 1½ cups.

FOR THE TORTAS:

 3 small zucchini, halved and sliced lengthwise
    about ½ inch thick
 Sixteen 8-inch flour tortillas, cut into thirty-two
    3-inch rounds (use a biscuit cutter or an inverted glass)

190

Olive oil for brushing the zucchini and tortillas

1 cup Spicy Hummus

8 ounces goat cheese

1 cup grated Monterey Jack cheese

1 cup grated white Cheddar cheese

2 jalapeño peppers, finely diced

1 large red onion, finely chopped

3 tablespoons ancho chile powder (see Note 2)

Kosher salt and freshly ground pepper

Preheat a gas or charcoal grill to high.

Brush the zucchini with olive oil and grill until softened, 1 minute on each side. Cut into julienne (small matchstick-size pieces).

Place 16 tortilla rounds on a work surface, spread with the hummus, and top with the zucchini. Crumble the goat cheese over the top and season with salt and pepper.

Place 8 tortilla rounds on the work surface and top with the Monterey Jack and Cheddar cheeses, jalapeño, and red onion. Season with salt and pepper. Place the 8 cheese-topped tortillas on top of 8 of the hummus-topped tortillas. Cover with the remaining 8 hummus-topped tortillas. Top with the 8 remaining tortillas.

Brush the tortas with oil and sprinkle with ancho chile powder. Grill oiled-side down until golden brown, 2 to 3 minutes. Brush with oil, sprinkle with ancho powder, turn over, and grill until the other side is golden brown and the cheese has melted, another 2 to 3 minutes.

NOTES:

1. To oven-roast a head of garlic, first cut off the top. Rub the garlic with olive oil and sprinkle with salt and pepper, wrap it in foil, and place it on a baking sheet. Roast at 300°F until soft, about 45 minutes.

2. Canned chipotle peppers in adobo and ancho chile powder are available at Hispanic or gourmet markets, or from Kitchen Market, 218 Eighth Avenue, New York, NY 10011, 212-243-4433, which has a mail-order list.

191

Grilled Ratatouille

MAKES 8 SERVINGS

The grill provides an efficient way to make the classic Provençale combination of ripe, fresh vegetables—and the results are spectacular. You can grill all the vegetables ahead and combine them at the last minute with some fragrant garlic and chopped herbs.

2 medium zucchini, halved lengthwise

2 medium yellow summer squash, halved lengthwise

2 Asian eggplants, halved lengthwise

2 medium red bell peppers, stemmed, seeded, and quartered

2 medium yellow bell peppers, stemmed, seeded, and quartered

2 medium red onions, quartered

1 basket cherry tomatoes (12 to 16)

½ cup plus 2 tablespoons olive oil

Kosher salt and freshly ground pepper

4 cloves garlic, finely chopped

3 tablespoons finely chopped oregano

¼ cup finely chopped flat-leaf parsley

Preheat a gas or charcoal grill to medium high.

Place the zucchini, yellow squash, eggplants, bell peppers, onions, and tomatoes in a large, shallow pan or baking dish, add ½ cup of the olive oil, and toss to coat. Season with salt and pepper. Grill the vegetables for 5 to 6 minutes with the grill uncovered, turning halfway through the cooking time. Remove the tomatoes, cover the grill, and cook the remaining vegetables until almost cooked through, about 2 minutes. Put the tomatoes in a large bowl.

Transfer vegetables to a cutting board and chop coarsely. Combine them with the tomatoes, add the remaining 2 tablespoons of olive oil, garlic, oregano, and parsley, and add salt and pepper. Serve warm or at room temperature.

Asparagus with Parmesan Cheese and Prosciutto

MAKES 8 SERVINGS

When you find beautiful asparagus at the farmers' market, trim the stems, toss with olive oil, sprinkle with salt and pepper, and throw them on the grill. Then dress them up with some Parmesan cheese and prosciutto, along with a citric vinaigrette, when you serve. It's helpful to grill them in a basket so they don't fall through the grate.

FOR THE LEMON-CAPER VINAIGRETTE:

¼ cup fresh lemon juice

½ cup olive oil

3 tablespoons capers

2 tablespoons finely chopped parsley

Freshly ground black pepper

Whisk together the lemon juice and olive oil in a small bowl. Add the capers and parsley and season with black pepper. May be refrigerated for 1 day; serve at room temperature. Makes about ¾ cup.

FOR THE ASPARAGUS:

24 asparagus spears, trimmed and peeled

2 tablespoons extra-virgin olive oil

Kosher salt and freshly ground pepper

8 thin slices prosciutto

Lemon-Caper Vinaigrette

Thinly shaved slices of Parmesan cheese

(continued)

Preheat a gas or charcoal grill to high.

Toss the asparagus with the olive oil, season with salt and pepper, and grill 2 to 3 minutes on each side. Wrap a piece of prosciutto around 3 asparagus spears and place on a platter; repeat with the remaining asparagus and prosciutto. Drizzle with the Lemon-Caper Vinaigrette and top with the Parmesan cheese.

GRILLED ASPARAGUS RISOTTO WITH WHITE TRUFFLE OIL

MAKES 8 SERVINGS

You can cook risotto on the grill, stirring fast over high heat the way I do, or cook it on the stove, if you're more comfortable doing it that way. Grill the asparagus ahead of time (using a basket, if you like), chop it up, and fold it into the rice. Add white truffle oil and you have a great summertime risotto.

FOR THE ASPARAGUS:

20 stalks asparagus, trimmed and peeled
Olive oil for brushing the asparagus
Kosher salt and freshly ground pepper

Preheat a gas or charcoal grill to high.

Brush the asparagus with olive oil and season with salt and pepper. Grill until just cooked through, 2 to 3 minutes on each side. Do not overcook. Cut on the bias into 1-inch pieces.

FOR THE RISOTTO:

- **8 to 10 cups homemade or canned vegetable stock**
- **3 tablespoons olive oil**
- **3 tablespoons unsalted butter**
- **1 cup finely chopped Spanish onion**
- **3 cloves garlic, finely chopped**
- **3 cups arborio rice**
- **1 cup dry white wine**
- **¼ cup finely chopped flat-leaf parsley**
- **Kosher salt and freshly ground pepper**
- **2 tablespoons white truffle oil**
- **8 slices thinly shaved Parmesan cheese**

Place the stock in a medium saucepan and bring to a simmer on the preheated hot grill, a side burner, or the stove. Using any of these heat sources, heat the olive oil and butter in a large saucepan until the butter has melted. Add the onion and cook until soft, about 5 minutes. Add the garlic and continue cooking 2 minutes. Add the rice, stir well to coat with the butter and oil mixture, and cook 1 minute. Add the wine and cook until evaporated.

Add 2 cups of stock to the rice, stirring constantly. When all the liquid has been absorbed, continue adding more in 2-cup increments until absorbed and the rice is al dente. It is important to keep the heat high and to stir constantly.

Fold in the asparagus and parsley and season with salt and pepper. Pile on a platter, drizzle with the white truffle oil, and top with the Parmesan cheese. Serve immediately.

195

GRILLED YELLOW TOMATO–YELLOW PEPPER SOUP WITH TORN CORN TORTILLAS

MAKES 8 SERVINGS

Quickly grill the delicate yellow tomatoes and the yellow bell peppers for this soup, keeping them on the fire just long enough to add a little flavor. You want them to keep their freshness and not be overcooked. Tear the tortillas into rough shapes and fry—they look really cool that way.

FOR THE TORN CORN TORTILLAS:

2 cups peanut oil
Two 8-inch blue corn tortillas, torn into bite-size pieces
Two 8-inch yellow corn tortillas, torn into bite-size pieces

Heat the peanut oil to 360°F, or until a piece of tortilla sizzles on contact, in a medium saucepan over medium heat. Fry the tortillas until crisp, about 30 seconds, and drain on paper towels.

FOR THE YELLOW TOMATO–YELLOW PEPPER SOUP:

2 medium yellow bell peppers

Olive oil for rubbing peppers and tomatoes,
    plus 3 tablespoons

1 medium red onion, finely chopped

2 cloves garlic, minced

2 cups dry white wine

8 medium yellow tomatoes, halved and seeded

¼ cup lime juice

¼ cup coarsely chopped basil

1 teaspoon cayenne

Kosher salt and freshly ground pepper

Torn Corn Tortillas

Basil chiffonade (fine ribbons) for garnish

Chopped cilantro, for garnish

Preheat a gas or charcoal grill to high.

Rub the peppers with olive oil and grill, turning, until charred on all sides, 3 to 5 minutes. Seed the peppers and coarsely chop.

In a saucepan over medium heat (on a side burner or on the stove), heat 3 tablespoons of olive oil until almost smoking and sweat the onion and garlic until translucent, about 5 minutes. Raise the heat to high, add the wine, and bring to a boil. Cook until the wine has completely evaporated, 5 to 10 minutes.

While the wine is reducing, rub the tomatoes with olive oil and grill until just cooked through, about 2 minutes on each side. Chop coarsely.

Once the wine has evaporated, reduce the heat to low, add the tomatoes and peppers, and cook 20 minutes, stirring occasionally. Add the lime juice, and process to a puree with a hand-held blender or in a food processor. Add the basil and cayenne and season with salt and pepper.

Pour into a large serving bowl and garnish with the Torn Corn Tortillas, basil, and cilantro.

197

Charred Corn Polenta with Grilled Tomato Vinaigrette

MAKES 8 SERVINGS

The corn kernels you fold into this polenta have been slightly charred on the grill, to release their sweet flavor and add a touch of smokiness. They release the subtle hints of corn in the polenta, bringing new complexity to a simple dish. The tomato vinaigrette adds its own grilled flavor, along with a bit of acidity.

FOR THE GRILLED TOMATO VINAIGRETTE:

4 ripe plum tomatoes

1 tablespoon plus ¾ cup olive oil

Kosher salt and freshly ground pepper

2 cloves garlic

2 tablespoons coarsely chopped red onion

¼ cup balsamic vinegar

2 tablespoons basil, chiffonade (see Note)

Preheat a gas or charcoal grill to high.

Toss the tomatoes with 1 tablespoon olive oil and season with salt and pepper. Grill just until the skins are blackened, remove from the grill, and chop coarsely. Place the tomatoes in a blender, add the garlic, onion, vinegar, and basil, and blend until smooth. With the motor running, slowly add the ¾ cup olive oil and blend until emulsified. Season with salt and pepper. May be refrigerated for 1 day; serve at room temperature. Makes about 2 cups.

FOR THE POLENTA:

2 ears of corn

8 cups chicken stock or water

2 cups finely ground yellow cornmeal

1 cup freshly grated Parmesan cheese

2 tablespoons finely chopped fresh parsley

Kosher salt and freshly ground pepper

Olive oil for brushing the polenta

Grilled Tomato Vinaigrette

At least 4 hours before serving, preheat a gas or charcoal grill to high.

In a medium pot of boiling salted water, blanch the corn about 5 minutes, until not quite cooked through. Place the ears on the grill until slightly charred on all sides, about 2 minutes. Remove from the grill and with a sharp knife, scrape the kernels into a medium bowl, or stand each ear on a cutting surface and scrape downward to remove the kernels. There should be about 1 cup.

Generously butter a large shallow baking dish (9 by 13 inches) and set aside.

Place the chicken stock or water in a large saucepan over high heat and bring to a boil. Slowly add the cornmeal, whisking constantly until well mixed. Reduce the heat to low and cook until thickened and smooth, stirring constantly, 12 to 15 minutes. Fold in the charred corn, Parmesan cheese, and parsley, season with salt and pepper, and pour into the buttered baking dish. Refrigerate, covered, 4 hours or overnight.

Preheat a gas or charcoal grill to high.

Cut the polenta into 2-inch circles or squares, brush with olive oil on both sides, and season with salt and pepper. Grill until golden brown, 2 to 3 minutes on each side.

Place on a large platter and drizzle with vinaigrette. Serve any extra vinaigrette on the side.

NOTE: To cut basil into chiffonade, or fine ribbons, roll up the leaves and cut into thin strips.

199

VEGETABLES

Grilled Corn and Sweet Onion Salad

MAKES 8 SERVINGS

I serve Vidalia onions all summer long, throughout their season. They add delicious sweetness and crunch to a salad of grilled summer corn. Some other flavorful sweet onions you may want to try are Maui and Walla Walla.

12 ears of corn, husks and silk removed

½ cup olive oil, plus extra for brushing the corn

¼ cup aged sherry vinegar

1 tablespoon Dijon mustard

1 garlic clove, minced

2 large red bell peppers, diced

**1 large Vidalia onion, thinly sliced, or use a Maui
   or Walla Walla onion**

4 ripe plum tomatoes, finely chopped

1 jalapeño pepper, finely chopped

¼ cup finely chopped chives

Kosher salt and freshly ground pepper

Preheat a gas or charcoal grill to medium.

In a large pot of boiling water, over high heat, cook the corn 5 minutes, until barely tender. Brush with olive oil and grill until slightly charred on all sides, about 2 minutes. Remove from the grill and with a sharp knife, scrape the kernels into a medium bowl, or stand each ear on a cutting surface and scrape downward to remove the kernels.

Combine the vinegar, mustard, and garlic in a large bowl and slowly whisk in the remaining ½ cup of olive oil until emulsified. Add the corn kernels, bell peppers, onion, tomatoes, jalapeño, and chives, and toss to coat with the dressing. Season with salt and pepper.

200

CORN NIBLETS WITH LIME BUTTER AND TARRAGON

MAKES 8 SERVINGS

These are very different from the corn niblets that we all remember getting out of the freezer or a can. The corn is grilled, then the slightly charred kernels are cut off and cooked with pepper, tarragon, and butter in a heavy pan right on the grill.

16 ears corn, husks and silk removed
Olive oil for brushing the corn
1½ sticks unsalted butter, cut into quarters
Juice of 2 limes
2 teaspoons cracked black pepper
2 tablespoons finely chopped tarragon
Kosher salt

Preheat a gas or charcoal grill to medium.

In a large pot of boiling water over high heat, cook the corn 5 minutes, until barely tender. Brush with the olive oil, and grill until slightly charred on all sides, about 2 minutes. Remove from the grill and with a sharp knife, scrape the kernels into a medium bowl, or stand each ear on a cutting surface and scrape downward to remove the kernels.

In a saucepan over medium heat (on a side burner or on the stove), heat the butter until melted and golden brown and add the lime juice and pepper. Remove the pan from the heat, stir in the tarragon, add the corn, and toss to coat. Season with salt and pepper and spoon into a medium serving bowl.

201

CORN ON THE COB WITH RED CHILE–GREEN ONION BUTTER

MAKES 8 SERVINGS

The grill is wonderful, but it's not perfect, and it tends to dry out corn. Instead of cooking the ears entirely on the grill, steam or simmer them about three-quarters of the way through first; then put them on the grill to develop that special charred flavor. Rub the corn with Red Chile–Green Onion Butter just as you take it off, so the butter melts in and adds spicy flavor to every kernel.

FOR THE RED CHILE–GREEN ONION BUTTER:

- ½ pound (2 sticks) unsalted butter
- 2 tablespoons ancho chile powder (see Note)
- 2 cloves garlic, minced
- ¼ cup chopped green onions (white bulb and 3 inches of green)
- 2 tablespoons fresh lime juice
- Kosher salt and freshly ground pepper

In a food processor, combine the butter, ancho chile powder, garlic, green onions, and lime juice, and season with salt and pepper. Process until completely mixed.

Place a sheet of parchment or wax paper on a work surface. Form the butter into a roll about 1 inch in diameter and place it along the long side of the paper, leaving a border of 1 inch. Roll up the butter in the paper and refrigerate for 30 minutes or up to 3 days. The butter also may be frozen. Makes about 1½ cups.

FOR THE CORN:

16 ears of corn, husks and silk removed
Olive oil for brushing the corn
Kosher salt and freshly ground pepper
Red Chile–Green Onion Butter

Preheat a gas or charcoal grill to medium.

In a large pot of boiling water, over high heat, cook the corn 5 minutes, until barely tender. Brush with olive oil, season with salt and pepper, and grill until slightly charred on all sides, about 2 minutes. Place the corn on a serving platter and immediately brush it with the Red Chile–Green Onion Butter. Serve hot, with any extra butter on the side.

NOTE: Ancho chile powder is available at Hispanic or gourmet markets, or from Kitchen Market, 218 Eighth Avenue, New York, NY 10011, 212-243-4433, which has a mail-order list.

203

Grilled Radicchio and Goat Cheese Salad with a Balsamic-Honey Glaze

MAKES 8 SERVINGS

Grilling gives radicchio a great flavor and a slightly browned color. Because radicchio can be a little bitter, combine it with a sweet glaze. Serve the salad with tangy fresh goat cheese.

FOR THE BALSAMIC-HONEY GLAZE:

2 cups balsamic vinegar

1 tablespoon honey

Bring the vinegar to a boil in a medium saucepan over medium-high heat and simmer until reduced to ½ cup. Stir in the honey, mix well, and let cool at room temperature. May be refrigerated, covered, for 1 day; use at room temperature. Makes about ½ cup.

FOR THE GRILLED RADICCHIO:

4 medium heads of radicchio, washed, stems cut off, and quartered

4 tablespoons olive oil

Kosher salt and freshly ground pepper

4 medium heads endive, washed, stems cut off, and leaves separated

8 ounces goat cheese, crumbled

Balsamic-Honey Glaze

Extra-virgin olive oil, for garnish

Preheat a gas or charcoal grill to medium high.

Brush the radicchio with oil, season with salt and pepper, and grill until browned and slightly softened, about 2 minutes on each side.

Arrange the endive leaves around the border of a large platter. Place the radicchio in the center, top with the crumbled goat cheese, and drizzle with the Balsamic-Honey Glaze. Splash with some extra-virgin olive oil.

Grilled Red Onion and Cucumber Salad with Yogurt-Mint Dressing

MAKES 8 SERVINGS

Grilled onions very thinly sliced and crisp cucumbers combine into a simple salad to serve along with grilled meat or fish. Add some cool Yogurt-Mint Dressing and mix it all up.

FOR THE YOGURT-MINT DRESSING:

1 cup plain yogurt, drained (see Note 1)
1 tablespoon olive oil
2 tablespoons tahini
2 tablespoons fresh lemon juice
2 cloves garlic, finely chopped
¼ teaspoon cumin
¼ cup mint, chiffonade (see Note 2)
Kosher salt and freshly ground pepper

Whisk together the yogurt, olive oil, tahini, lemon juice, garlic, cumin, and mint in a medium bowl and season with salt and pepper. Let sit at room temperature for half an hour before serving, to blend the flavors. May be refrigerated for 1 day; serve at room temperature. Makes about 1 cup.

FOR THE RED ONION AND CUCUMBER SALAD:

**2 medium red onions, peeled and sliced
crosswise ½ inch thick**

Olive oil for brushing the onions

Kosher salt and freshly ground pepper

**3 cucumbers (preferably English seedless), peeled, halved
lengthwise, and sliced ½ inch thick**

3 tablespoons finely chopped fresh oregano

Yogurt-Mint Dressing

½ cup crumbled feta cheese

Preheat a gas or charcoal grill to high.

Brush both sides of the onion slices with olive oil and season with salt and pepper. Grill just to obtain grill marks and cook slightly, 2 to 3 minutes on each side.

Remove from the grill and chop coarsely. In a medium bowl, combine the onions, cucumber, and oregano and toss with the Yogurt-Mint Dressing. Season with salt and pepper and sprinkle with the feta cheese.

NOTES:

1. To drain yogurt, place it in a cheesecloth-lined strainer over a bowl for 1 hour, until thickened. Discard the liquid that remains in the bowl.

2. To cut mint into chiffonade, or fine ribbons, roll up the leaves and cut into thin strips.

Grilled Sweet Onion and Tomato Salad

MAKES 8 SERVINGS

Balsamic vinegar, olive oil, tomatoes, and onions are the four classic ingredients of a great vegetable salad. Grilling tomatoes gives them a lot of added flavor—they taste like the essence of summer. Use your favorite olive oil to finish the dish.

FOR THE ONIONS:

Eight ¼-inch slices Vidalia onion
Olive oil for brushing the onions

Preheat a gas or charcoal grill to medium high.

Brush the onions with olive oil and grill until marked and softened, 2 minutes on each side.

FOR THE BALSAMIC-MUSTARD VINAIGRETTE:

½ cup balsamic vinegar
1 tablespoon Dijon mustard
2 cloves garlic, finely chopped
½ cup extra-virgin olive oil
Kosher salt and freshly ground pepper

Whisk together the vinegar, mustard, garlic, and olive oil in a small bowl and season with salt and pepper. May be refrigerated for 1 day; use at room temperature. Makes 1 cup.

FOR THE SALAD:

Sixteen ¼-inch slices beefsteak tomato
Grilled Vidalia onions
6 cups watercress
1 cup Balsamic-Mustard Vinaigrette
½ cup packed basil, chiffonade (see Note)

Place 8 tomato slices on a work surface and top each with a slice of grilled onion. Cover with another slice of tomato.

Toss the watercress with ¼ cup of the vinaigrette and pile on a large platter.

Place the tomato stacks over the watercress and drizzle with the Balsamic-Mustard Vinaigrette. Sprinkle with the basil.

NOTE: To cut basil into chiffonade, or fine ribbons, roll up the leaves and cut into thin strips.

Grilled Cherry Tomato and Watercress Salad with Green Garlic Vinaigrette

MAKES 8 SERVINGS

Obviously, this is the dish that grilling baskets were invented for. Grill the cherry tomatoes just a little, and add the vinaigrette while they are still warm. The salad is gorgeous!

FOR THE GREEN GARLIC VINAIGRETTE:

2 green onions (white bulb and 3 inches of green), coarsely chopped
¼ cup parsley leaves
¼ cup spinach leaves
4 cloves garlic, coarsely chopped
¼ cup rice wine vinegar
½ cup extra-virgin olive oil
1 tablespoon honey
Kosher salt and freshly ground pepper

Combine the green onion, parsley, spinach, garlic, and vinegar in a blender and blend until smooth. With the motor running, slowly add the olive oil until mixture is emulsified. Add honey and season with salt and pepper. May be refrigerated for 1 day; serve at room temperature. Makes 1¼ cups.

FOR THE GRILLED CHERRY TOMATOES:

2 pounds cherry tomatoes, cut in half
2 tablespoons olive oil
Kosher salt and freshly ground pepper
1 pound watercress, cleaned
Green Garlic Vinaigrette

Preheat a gas or charcoal grill to high.

Toss the tomatoes with the olive oil in a medium bowl, and season with salt and pepper. On the grill or in a wire basket, grill the tomatoes until they are just cooked through but still hold their shape, 1 to 2 minutes on each side.

Toss the watercress with ¼ cup of the Green Garlic Vinaigrette, season with salt and pepper, and arrange on a platter. Top with the tomatoes and drizzle with more of the vinaigrette. Serve any remaining vinaigrette alongside.

211

Napa Cabbage and Sesame Seed Slaw

MAKES 8 SERVINGS

In contrast to red cabbage or regular green cabbage, napa is softer and has a more buttery flavor. Wasabi, a fiery Japanese horseradish, adds heat to this salad, the Asian notes of which pair well with Asian-style dishes.

FOR THE WASABI DRESSING:

- 2 teaspoons wasabi powder (available at Asian markets and some supermarkets)
- 1 tablespoon water
- 2 cloves garlic, finely chopped
- 1 tablespoon finely grated gingerroot
- 1 tablespoon fresh lime juice
- ⅓ cup rice wine vinegar
- ¼ cup peanut oil
- 1 tablespoon honey
- Kosher salt and freshly ground pepper

Combine the wasabi powder and water in a small bowl. Whisk in the garlic, ginger-root, lime juice, vinegar, oil, and honey and season with salt and pepper.

FOR THE SLAW:

1 large head napa cabbage, finely shredded

2 large carrots, peeled and finely shredded

4 green onions (white bulb and 3 inches of green), finely
   sliced on the bias

1 cup finely sliced snow peas (strings removed
   and sliced on the bias)

Wasabi Dressing

Kosher salt and finely ground pepper

1 tablespoon white sesame seeds, toasted (see Note)

1 tablespoon black sesame seeds

Combine the cabbage, carrots, green onions, and snow peas in a large bowl. Add the dressing and coat well. Season with salt and pepper and sprinkle with the sesame seeds.

NOTE: To toast sesame seeds, place a heavy, dry skillet over low heat and cook the seeds 2 to 3 minutes, tossing or stirring them so they don't burn. Remove from the heat as soon as they are toasted.

WILD MUSHROOMS WITH CRUSHED HAZELNUTS AND GARLIC

MAKES 8 SERVINGS

This savory mushroom dish is right out of Bolo. Grill portobellos, shiitakes, oyster mushrooms—as many kinds as you can find. Combine chopped hazelnuts with a mixture of chopped herbs, lemon zest, olive oil, and fresh garlic, and drizzle over the mushrooms while they are still warm.

FOR THE HAZELNUT MIXTURE:

- 1 cup finely chopped hazelnuts
- 2 tablespoons finely chopped thyme leaves
- 2 tablespoons finely chopped flat-leaf parsley (stems and leaves)
- 4 cloves garlic, finely chopped
- 1 tablespoon finely chopped lemon zest
- ¼ cup olive oil
- Kosher salt and freshly ground pepper

Combine the hazelnuts, thyme, parsely, garlic, lemon zest, and olive oil in a medium bowl and mix well. Season with salt and pepper. May be refrigerated, covered, for 1 day; serve at room temperature. Makes 1½ cups.

FOR THE GRILLED MUSHROOMS:

4 large portobello mushrooms, cleaned and stemmed

8 small shiitake mushrooms, cleaned and stemmed

8 oyster mushrooms, cleaned

Olive oil for brushing the mushrooms

Kosher salt and freshly ground pepper

Hazelnut mixture

Preheat a gas or charcoal grill to high.

Brush the mushrooms with olive oil and season with salt and pepper. Grill, turning, until just cooked through. The portobellos will take 4 to 5 minutes on each side; the shiitakes and oysters, 2 to 3 minutes on each side.

Remove the mushrooms from the grill as they are done. Slice the portobellos ½ inch thick and arrange in the middle of a large platter. Surround with shiitake and oyster mushrooms and drizzle with the hazelnut mixture. May be refrigerated, covered, for 1 day; serve at room temperature.

GRILLED MUSHROOM TACOS WITH WHITE TRUFFLE OIL

MAKES 8 SERVINGS

If you choose not to do this dish from scratch, you can work sorcery with leftovers. For a terrific variation of the real thing, just put yesterday's Wild Mushrooms with Crushed Hazelnuts and Garlic in flour tortillas, grill, and sprinkle with some white truffle oil.

White truffle oil is a very trendy ingredient, but it's popular for good reason: it gives you all the flavor of expensive truffles at a bargain price. Its musty perfume enhances many foods, especially mushrooms.

Olive oil for brushing the mushrooms and tortillas

12 cremini mushrooms, stemmed and cleaned

1 large portobello mushroom, stemmed and cleaned

Kosher salt and freshly ground pepper

Eight 6-inch corn tortillas (or cut 8-inch tortillas to size using a 6-inch plate as a guide)

10 cloves roasted garlic, pureed (see Note)

1 pound Italian fontina cheese, thinly sliced

3 tablespoons finely chopped fresh thyme leaves

3 tablespoons white truffle oil

Preheat a gas or charcoal grill to medium.

Brush the mushrooms with olive oil and season with salt and pepper. Grill until golden brown and cooked through, 2 to 3 minutes on each side for creminis, 3 to 4 minutes on each side for portobellos. Remove from the grill and chop coarsely.

Place the tortillas on a work surface and spread each with some of the garlic puree. Divide the cheese among the tortillas, top with the mushrooms, and sprinkle with the thyme. Fold each tortilla in half, over the filling, to make a semicircle. Brush the tops lightly with olive oil.

Grill, oiled-side down, until golden brown, about 3 minutes. Brush with olive oil, turn over carefully, and continue grilling until the tortillas are golden brown and the cheese has melted, 2 to 3 minutes. Place on a serving platter and drizzle with the white truffle oil.

NOTE: To oven-roast a head of garlic, first cut off the top. Rub the garlic with olive oil and sprinkle with salt and pepper, wrap it in foil, place it on a baking sheet, and roast at 300°F until soft, about 45 minutes.

VEGETABLES

Grilled Mushroom and Potato Salad with Dijon Mustard Dressing

MAKES 8 SERVINGS

For a simple but terrific salad, put earthy grilled wild mushrooms together with boiled potatoes, add crisp onion, bell pepper, and fresh herbs, and toss with a garlicky Dijon Mustard Vinaigrette. The potatoes must be dressed when warm, to absorb the flavors of the vinaigrette.

FOR THE DIJON MUSTARD VINAIGRETTE:

- ½ cup white wine vinegar
- 2 tablespoons good quality mayonnaise
- 2 tablespoons Dijon mustard
- 4 cloves garlic, finely chopped
- ¾ cup olive oil
- Kosher salt and freshly ground pepper

In a medium bowl, whisk together the vinegar, mayonnaise, mustard, and garlic until combined. Slowly add the olive oil and whisk until emulsified. Season with salt and pepper. May be refrigerated for 1 day. Serve at room temperature. Makes about 1½ cups.

FOR THE MUSHROOM AND POTATO SALAD:

- **8 large red potatoes**
- **4 large shiitake mushrooms**
- **2 large portobello mushrooms, stems removed**
- **Olive oil for brushing the mushrooms**
- **Kosher salt and freshly ground pepper**
- **1 large red onion, finely sliced**
- **2 red bell peppers, cut into julienne (small matchsticks)**
- **1 tablespoon finely chopped fresh thyme leaves**
- **¼ cup coarsely chopped flat-leaf parsley**

Preheat a gas or charcoal grill to high.

Brush the mushrooms with olive oil and season with salt and pepper. Grill until golden brown and cooked through, 3 to 4 minutes on each side. Slice thinly and place in a large bowl. Cover to keep warm.

In a large pot of boiling salted water over high heat, boil the potatoes until cooked but still firm to the touch, about 15 minutes. Cut the cooked potatoes into 1-inch cubes and add to the bowl. Add the onion and red peppers.

Pour the Dijon Mustard Vinaigrette over the warm potato mixture and mix gently to combine. Add the thyme and parsley and season with salt and pepper. Serve at room temperature.

219

TOASTED ISRAELI COUSCOUS SALAD WITH GRILLED SUMMER VEGETABLES

MAKES 8 SERVINGS

Israeli couscous is a pearl-like pasta, larger and smoother than regular couscous, that makes an excellent canvas for Balsamic-Garlic Vinaigrette and crunchy grilled vegetables. This is a luscious salad, with lots of great textures running through it.

FOR THE BALSAMIC-GARLIC VINAIGRETTE:

½ cup balsamic vinegar

1 tablespoon Dijon mustard

2 cloves garlic, coarsely chopped

1 cup olive oil

Kosher salt and freshly ground pepper

In a small bowl, whisk together the vinegar, mustard, and garlic. Slowly add the olive oil and whisk until combined. Season with salt and pepper. May be refrigerated, covered or in a squeeze bottle, for 1 day; serve at room temperature. Makes 1½ cups.

FOR THE ISRAELI COUSCOUS:

3 tablespoons olive oil

1 pound Israeli couscous

6 cups lightly salted vegetable stock or water
    (or enough to cover the couscous), heated to a simmer

Kosher salt and freshly ground pepper

Heat the olive oil until almost smoking in a small pot over medium-high heat and toast the couscous until lightly golden brown. Cover with the hot stock, bring to a boil, and cook until al dente, 5 to 6 minutes. If necessary, drain well and place in a large serving bowl. Season with salt and pepper.

FOR THE GRILLED SUMMER VEGETABLES:

2 medium green zucchini, quartered lengthwise

2 medium yellow zucchini, quartered lengthwise

10 asparagus spears, trimmed and peeled

12 cherry tomatoes

1 red bell pepper, quartered and seeded

1 yellow bell pepper, quartered and seeded

Kosher salt and freshly ground pepper

¼ cup basil, chiffonade (see Note)

¼ cup coarsely chopped flat-leaf parsley

Preheat the grill to high.

Place the green and yellow zucchini, asparagus, tomatoes, and red and yellow bell peppers in a large bowl and pour half the vinaigrette over them. Let sit at room temperature for 15 minutes.

Remove the vegetables from the marinade, shaking off the excess (discard the used marinade). Season with salt and pepper, and grill, turning, until just cooked through, about 4 minutes for the zucchini, 3 minutes for the asparagus, 2 minutes for the cherry tomatoes, and 6 minutes for the bell peppers.

Cut the zucchini and peppers into ½-inch pieces. Cut asparagus on the bias into ½-inch pieces. Cut the tomatoes in half. Add the vegetables to the couscous, add the basil and parsley, and toss with the remaining vinaigrette. Season with salt and pepper. Serve at room temperature.

NOTE: To cut basil leaves into chiffonade, or fine ribbons, roll up and cut into thin strips.

221

VEGETABLES

New Potato and Smoked Salmon Salad with Mustard–Fresh Dill Dressing

MAKES 8 SERVINGS

When you add smoked salmon to grilled new potatoes and drizzle on some Mustard–Fresh Dill Dressing, there are all your Sunday brunch flavors—you don't need anything else. Serve Bloody Marys and mimosas, and let the festivities go on until it's time to wind up the weekend and start cleaning the house.

FOR THE MUSTARD–FRESH DILL DRESSING:

- ½ cup sour cream
- 2 tablespoons whole grain mustard
- 2 tablespoons Dijon mustard
- 2 teaspoons fresh lemon juice
- 2 tablespoons finely chopped fresh dill
- Kosher salt and freshly ground pepper

In a small bowl, combine the sour cream, mustards, lemon juice, and dill, and mix well. Season with salt and pepper. May be refrigerated for 1 day; serve at room temperature. Makes about ¾ cup.

FOR THE NEW POTATO AND SMOKED SALMON SALAD:

2 pounds new potatoes (16 to 20 small)

2 tablespoons fresh lemon juice

¼ cup olive oil

4 cloves garlic, minced

Kosher salt and freshly ground pepper

4 green onions (white bulb and 3 inches of green),
    finely sliced

¼ cup flat-leaf parsley

2 tablespoons capers, drained

10 slices smoked salmon, coarsely chopped

2 tablespoons coarsely chopped dill

Mustard–Fresh Dill Dressing

Cook the new potatoes in a large pot of boiling salted water over high heat until tender, 12 to 15 minutes. Drain, slice ¼ inch thick, and place in a large bowl.

Whisk together the lemon juice, olive oil, and garlic in a small bowl. Season with salt and pepper.

Add the green onions, parsley, and capers to the potatoes. Add the lemon-olive oil-garlic vinaigrette and toss to coat. Season with salt and pepper.

In a large bowl, gently fold the smoked salmon into the potato salad. Garnish with the dill and drizzle with the Mustard–Fresh Dill Dressing.

223

Warm Potato and Sweet Onion Salad with Bacon Dressing

MAKES 8 SERVINGS

This is a perfect dish to serve when there is a hint of a chill in the air and it's starting to get dark a little early. The warm salad of potatoes, onions, and bacon dressing will remind you of having lunch at a Paris bistro, sitting at an outdoor table, people-watching. Use the bacon fat to sauté the onion and garlic, in traditional bistro style.

2 pounds new potatoes (16 to 20 small)

1 tablespoon olive oil

8 slices bacon, uncooked, coarsely chopped

1 large Vidalia onion, thinly sliced

2 small garlic cloves, minced

¾ cup white wine vinegar

2 teaspoons finely chopped thyme leaves

¼ cup coarsely chopped flat-leaf parsley

Kosher salt and freshly ground pepper

Cook the new potatoes in a large pot of boiling salted water over high heat until tender, 10 to 15 minutes. Drain, cut into quarters, and place in a large bowl.

Heat the oil until almost smoking in a medium skillet over medium heat and cook the bacon until golden brown and crisp and the fat has rendered. Remove the bacon to a paper towel–lined plate and pour off all but 3 tablespoons of the fat. Add the onion to the skillet and sauté until lightly golden brown, 4 to 5 minutes. Add the garlic and cook for 2 more minutes. Add the vinegar, drained bacon, thyme, and parsley and season with salt and pepper.

Pour the bacon mixture over the potatoes and mix gently. Season to taste.

MESA GRILL POTATO SALAD

MAKES 8 SERVINGS

An oldie but a goodie, this is one of the most requested dishes at Mesa Grill. Serve it alongside grilled fish or chicken, or on its own. Use the smallest new potatoes you can find—they will have the creamiest texture.

2 pounds new potatoes (16 to 20 small)

2 cups prepared mayonnaise

¼ cup Dijon mustard

1 tablespoon pureed canned chipotles (see Notes 1 and 2)

2 tablespoons fresh lime juice

2 green onions (white bulb and 3 inches of green), finely chopped

1 medium red onion, thinly sliced

1 jalapeño pepper, finely diced

4 cloves garlic, finely chopped

3 tablespoons coarsely chopped cilantro

½ teaspoon cayenne

Kosher salt and freshly ground pepper

In a large pot of boiling salted water over high heat, boil the potatoes until cooked through, 12 to 15 minutes. Drain and slice ½ inch thick.

In a medium bowl, combine the mayonnaise, mustard, chipotle puree, lime juice, green and red onions, jalapeño, garlic, cilantro, cayenne, salt, and pepper. Place the warm potatoes in a large bowl and pour the mixture over them. Mix well and season to taste with additional salt and pepper.

NOTES:

1. Canned chipotle peppers in adobo are available at Hispanic or gourmet markets or mail order from Kitchen Market, 218 Eighth Avenue, New York, NY 10011, 212-243-4433.

2. To make chipotle puree, process canned chipotles in a blender or a food processor, along with a little of their liquid.

GRILLED SWEET POTATO AND GREEN ONION SALAD

MAKES 8 SERVINGS

You've had white potato salad, now try sweet potatoes. They have deep color, great texture, and an earthy sweetness. Oil and grill them, chop them, and add green onions—a whole bunch. This is a totally beautiful salad.

4 medium sweet potatoes (about 1 pound each), peeled and cut into ½ inch slices

1 bunch green onions (white bulb and 3 inches of green)

½ cup olive oil, plus extra for brushing the potatoes and green onions

1 tablespoon Dijon mustard

¼ cup cider vinegar

¼ cup balsamic vinegar

1 tablespoon honey

Kosher salt and freshly ground pepper

¼ cup coarsely chopped flat-leaf parsley

Preheat a gas or charcoal grill to medium.

Brush the potatoes and green onions with olive oil. Grill the potatoes until tender, 4 minutes on each side; grill the green onions until softened and marked, 2 to 3 minutes on each side. When cool enough to handle, cut the potatoes into 1-inch cubes and finely chop the green onions.

In a large bowl, whisk together the remaining ½ cup olive oil, the mustard, vinegars, and honey, and season with salt and pepper. Add the potatoes, green onions, and parsley and mix until the potatoes are coated with the dressing. Season to taste with additional salt and pepper.

Spicy Hummus Dip with Grilled Pita and Vegetables

MAKES 8 SERVINGS

I love eating hummus, but for me, the perfect version is one with a little spice, so I pump it up with a burst of chipotle. This is a really good starter before the main course. For the dip, double the recipe for Spicy Hummus that appears with Grilled Zucchini and Goat Cheese Tortas (but you don't have to double the chipotle pepper).

FOR THE GRILLED PITA AND VEGETABLES:

6 pita breads

Olive oil for brushing the pita

1 yellow bell pepper, seeded and cut lengthwise into eighths

1 red bell pepper, seeded and cut lengthwise into eighths

1 purple bell pepper, seeded and cut lengthwise into eighths

Double recipe of Spicy Hummus (it is not necessary to double the chipotle pepper) (page 190)

Preheat a gas or charcoal grill to medium high.

Brush the pita with oil on both sides and grill until golden brown.

Serve the Spicy Hummus Dip in a bowl surrounded by the pita and vegetables.

Prosciutto-Wrapped Grilled Figs with Buffalo Mozzarella and Rosemary Oil

MAKES 8 SERVINGS

This is the perfect appetizer, offering a new take on classic prosciutto-wrapped figs. Fresh buffalo mozzarella is incredibly tender, milky, and moist, and it's highlighted by the savory, smoky grilled prosciutto and aromatic Rosemary Oil.

FOR THE ROSEMARY OIL:

¼ cup fresh rosemary leaves

2 tablespoons coarsely chopped chives

1 cup olive oil

Kosher salt and freshly ground pepper

Place the rosemary, chives, and oil in a blender and blend until smooth. Strain, and season with salt and pepper. May be refrigerated for 1 day; serve at room temperature. Makes about 1 cup.

FOR THE FIGS:

8 fresh figs, halved lengthwise

16 thin slices buffalo mozzarella, about 2 inches square

16 thin slices prosciutto

16 toothpicks, soaked in water for 1 hour

Kosher salt and freshly ground pepper

1 cup Rosemary Oil

228

Preheat a gas or charcoal grill to high.

On a work surface, place 1 slice of cheese on the cut side of each fig. Wrap with a slice of prosciutto and secure with a toothpick. Brush with Rosemary Oil and season with salt and pepper.

Grill cut-side down for 2 minutes; turn over and continue cooking until the figs are almost cooked through and the cheese has melted, 2 to 3 minutes.

Place the figs on a serving platter and immediately drizzle with Rosemary Oil.

Grilled Crudités with Cabrales Blue Cheese

MAKES 8 SERVINGS

These vegetables are lightly grilled so they remain crisp, like crudités, but they have an extra smoky dimension given by the grill. A grill basket is a good idea for cooking them.

FOR THE CABRALES BLUE CHEESE DIP:

2 cups crème fraîche (see Note 1)

2 tablespoons chipotle puree (see Note 2)

½ cup finely crumbled Cabrales blue cheese

Kosher salt and freshly ground pepper

Combine the crème fraîche and chipotle puree in a medium bowl and mix well. Add the cheese and season with salt and pepper. May be refrigerated, covered, for 1 day. Makes about 2½ cups.

FOR THE CRUDITÉS:

2 cups olive oil

3 tablespoons coarsely chopped fresh thyme leaves

Kosher salt and freshly ground pepper

16 baby carrots, cleaned

1 large fennel bulb, peeled and sliced lengthwise ½ inch thick

8 pattypan squash

8 baby zucchini, quartered lengthwise

16 asparagus spears, trimmed and peeled

230

2 red bell peppers, stemmed, quartered, and seeded

2 yellow bell peppers, stemmed, quartered, and seeded

2 poblano peppers, halved and seeded

Kosher salt and freshly ground pepper

Preheat a gas or charcoal grill to medium high.

Combine the olive oil and thyme in a large baking dish and toss the vegetables in the oil to coat. Season with salt and pepper. Grill, turning, until the vegetables are just cooked through, but still hold their shapes. They will finish at different times, so take them off the grill as they are done and let the others continue cooking. None will need more than 3 to 4 minutes of grilling.

Arrange on a large platter and serve a bowl of Cabrales Blue Cheese Dip alongside.

NOTES:

1. To make 2 cups crème fraîche, combine 2 cups heavy cream and 4 tablespoons buttermilk and let sit at room temperature, covered, until thick (8 to 24 hours). May be refrigerated up to 10 days.

2. To make chipotle puree, process canned chipotles in a blender or food processor, along with a little of their liquid.

7. SWEET THINGS

**M**y assistant, Stephanie Banyas (who seems to live on dessert alone), helped me work out the dessert ideas for *Boy Meets Grill*. We thought about what dishes would provide the happiest endings to these informal, often al fresco meals. I wanted them to be refreshing, to go well with the grilled foods that preceded them, and to be fun and easy.

Fresh fruit preparations topped my list. White peaches made into a home-style buckle, mangoes baked under a crisp mantle of coconut and macadamia nuts, a comfortably old-fashioned pudding cake flavored with Key lime, blueberries providing the bottom/top layer of an upside-down cake, peaches in a buttery pie served with homemade ice cream, a meringue-topped banana split pie, and a fruit salad of watermelon, grilled peaches, and sweet blackberries—these are the treats you want for a grilling party.

For the chocoholoc kid in everyone, pass around Chocolate-Raspberry "Fudgesicles," or serve generous wedges of White Chocolate–Banana Cream–Coconut Pie.

Something icy and sweet is always welcome after a sizzling meal. Among the coolest desserts on earth are deep, rich Frozen Mocha Cooler, and that easiest one of all, really good vanilla ice cream swirled with ripe crushed blackberries.

233

Mango-Coconut Macadamia Crisp

MAKES 8 SERVINGS

This isn't Grandma's fruit crisp. A filling of ripe mangoes is mellowed by rich dark rum and a touch of ginger, and topped with macadamia nuts and crisp coconut.

FOR THE MANGO FILLING:

¼ cup dark rum

½ cup light brown sugar

2 tablespoons finely chopped crystallized ginger

Juice of 1 lemon

2 ripe mangoes, peeled, pitted, and cut into 1-inch chunks

Combine the rum, brown sugar, and ginger in a small saucepan over medium heat and cook, stirring, until the sugar dissolves and the mixture comes to a simmer. Reduce the heat to low and simmer 5 to 6 minutes.

Place the mangoes and lemon juice in a bowl and stir to combine. Add the rum mixture and mix well.

FOR THE CRUMB TOPPING:

¼ pound (1 stick) unsalted butter, cut into ½-inch cubes
½ cup light brown sugar
½ cup all-purpose flour
1 teaspoon ground cinnamon

Place all the ingredients in a medium bowl and, using a hand-held mixer, mix until crumbly, 1 to 2 minutes.

TO ASSEMBLE:

Butter for greasing the baking dish
Mango Filling
Crumb Topping
½ cup coarsely chopped macadamia nuts
¼ cup unsweetened coconut

Preheat the oven to 350°F. Butter a 9-by-9-by-2-inch baking dish.

Pour the mango filling into the prepared pan and spread evenly with a knife. Sprinkle the crumb topping over it and top with the nuts and coconut. Bake until juices bubble and top is golden brown, 40 to 45 minutes. Let cool to room temperature.

White Peach Melba Buckle

MAKES 8 SERVINGS

This buckle (a simple fruit-filled cake) is the perfect summer dessert, with its pockets of fresh, juicy peaches and its crumbly nut-and-sugar topping. The optional Framboise, a raspberry liqueur, intensifies its flavors. When you want a dish that showcases seasonal fruit and lets you eat cake, as well, this is a good one to try.

FOR THE RASPBERRY SAUCE:

1 pint fresh raspberries

3 tablespoons sugar, or more to taste

1 tablespoon fresh lemon juice

1 tablespoon Framboise (optional)

Place all the ingredients in a food processor and process until smooth. Strain into a small bowl. May be refrigerated for 1 day. Makes about 1 cup.

FOR THE CRUMB TOPPING:

4 tablespoons (½ stick) cold unsalted butter, cut into small pieces

¼ cup sugar

2 tablespoons light brown sugar

¼ teaspoon cinnamon

¼ teaspoon freshly grated nutmeg

In a small bowl, using a pastry blender or two knives, mix all the ingredients together until the mixture is coarsely crumbled.

FOR THE CAKE:

¾ cup unsalted butter (1½ sticks), softened

¾ cup sugar

1 teaspoon pure vanilla extract

¼ teaspoon almond extract

3 large eggs

1 cup cake flour

1½ teaspoons baking powder

Pinch of salt

6 large, ripe white peaches (3 to 4 pounds) peeled,
   pitted, and cut into ¼-inch slices

1 pint fresh raspberries

Crumb Topping

¼ cup slivered almonds

1 quart vanilla ice cream

Raspberry Sauce

Preheat the oven to 350°F. Butter an 8-inch square baking dish or an 11-inch gratin dish.

Mix the butter and sugar in the bowl of a standing electric mixer until light and fluffy. Add the vanilla and almond extracts and beat 1 minute. Add the eggs one at a time, beating until each is incorporated.

Sift together the flour, baking powder, and salt and add to the butter mixture, mixing until just combined. Do not overmix. Gently fold the peaches and raspberries into the batter and scrape into the prepared dish. Sprinkle the crumb topping evenly over the batter, then sprinkle the almonds over the crumb mixture.

Bake until the cake is lightly golden and has set, 40 to 45 minutes. Let cool slightly on a rack for no more than 15 minutes—it is best served warm. Cut into large squares and serve with vanilla ice cream and Raspberry Sauce.

237

Chocolate-Raspberry "Fudgesicles"

MAKES 8 SERVINGS

Do you remember the Fudgesicles you loved when you were a kid? They were fudgy tasting, with a frozen, chewy consistency. That's what these are like, and they bring back my childhood summer days, standing in front of the ice-cream truck with a bunch of other kids. (The subtle kick of Chambord is a bonus for grown-ups.)

2 cups whole milk

¾ cup sugar

5 large egg yolks

8 ounces bittersweet chocolate, finely chopped
   (Callebaut, if possible)

1 teaspoon vanilla extract

1 tablespoon Chambord

2 cups heavy cream

2 cups fresh raspberries

4 ounces white chocolate, coarsely chopped
   (Callebaut, if possible)

8 paper or Styrofoam cups or juice-drink boxes

8 wooden popsicle sticks

In a medium saucepan over medium-high heat, bring the milk and ½ cup sugar to a boil; reduce the heat to low and simmer until the sugar has melted, 2 to 3 minutes.

Meanwhile, in a medium bowl, whisk the egg yolks with the remaining ¼ cup sugar until thick and light in color. Add one-third of the hot milk to the yolk mixture, whisking constantly. Pour this back into the saucepan with the remaining milk. Cook the custard over medium heat, stirring constantly, until it coats the back of a wooden spoon. Do not allow the mixture to boil.

Remove from the heat and stir in 4 ounces of the chopped bittersweet chocolate, until well blended. Pour into a medium bowl set in a larger bowl of ice water and stir until cool. Stir in the vanilla, Chambord, and heavy cream. Place in freezer, covered, until semifrozen, 2½ to 3 hours.

Place the raspberries on a baking sheet in an even layer and freeze for at least 1 hour.

When the chocolate custard is semifrozen, beat with a hand-held mixer until fluffy. Immediately fold in the remaining bittersweet chocolate, the white chocolate, and the frozen raspberries. Spoon into the cups and insert popsicle sticks into the center. Freeze for at least 3 hours, or overnight. (The paper or Styrofoam will peel off easily.)

Frozen Mocha Cooler

MAKES 8 SERVINGS

A perfect ending to a hot day, not to mention a hot, grilled dinner, this dessert is paradise for iced-coffee lovers.

6 cups strong hot espresso (about 36 ounces)

1 to 1½ cups sugar, plus 2 tablespoons for the whipped cream

4 tablespoons unsweetened Dutch process cocoa powder

2 cups half-and-half or milk

6 to 8 cups crushed ice

1 cup very cold heavy cream

1 teaspoon vanilla extract

6 ounces bittersweet chocolate, finely grated

Place the hot espresso in a medium bowl and sweeten with sugar to taste. Whisk in the cocoa powder until smooth. Add the half-and-half or milk, combine well, and refrigerate until cool, about 1 hour.

(continued)

239

Place one-fourth of the espresso mixture and one-fourth of the ice in a blender and blend until smooth and thick, adding more ice if necessary. Remove to a bowl and place in the freezer to keep cool. Repeat in batches with the remaining mixture, and add to the mixture in the bowl.

Place the heavy cream, 2 tablespoons of sugar, and vanilla extract in a medium bowl and beat to soft peaks with a hand-held mixer.

Spoon espresso-chocolate mixture into 8 glass Irish coffee mugs and top with whipped cream and shaved chocolate. Serve with spoons and straws.

LEMON-BLUEBERRY UPSIDE-DOWN CAKE

MAKES 8 SERVINGS

My favorite dessert for blueberry season, this recipe expands the range way beyond pies and muffins, with an upside-down caramelized blueberry topping melting over the luscious white chocolate and coconut-flavored cake beneath.

FOR THE LEMON-BLUEBERRY TOPPING:

4 tablespoons unsalted butter, cut into 4 pieces
⅔ cup tightly packed light brown sugar
2 cups fresh blueberries
2 teaspoons grated lemon zest

Preheat the oven to 350°F.

In a 9-inch round cake pan, melt the butter over low heat. Stir in the brown sugar and cook, stirring, until the mixture is smooth and bubbling, 3 to 4 minutes. Remove the pan from the heat.

Arrange the blueberries evenly over the brown sugar mixture. Scatter the lemon zest over the blueberries.

FOR THE CAKE BATTER:

1⅓ cups all-purpose flour

1½ teaspoons double-acting baking powder

Pinch of salt

½ cup (1 stick) unsalted butter, softened

1 cup sugar

2 large eggs, at room temperature

1½ teaspoons vanilla extract

½ cup unsweetened coconut milk

2 ounces white chocolate, coarsely chopped (Callebaut, if possible)

Sift the flour, baking powder, and salt onto a piece of wax paper or into a bowl.

In a large bowl, using a hand-held mixer set at medium speed, beat the butter until creamy, about 30 seconds. Add the sugar and continue to beat until the mixture is light in texture and color, 2 to 3 minutes. Beat in the eggs one at a time. Beat in the vanilla and white chocolate.

On low speed, beat in half the flour mixture until just combined. Scrape down the sides of the bowl. Beat in the coconut milk, then beat in the remaining flour mixture until combined.

Spoon the batter over the topping in the cake pan, spreading it evenly over the berries and covering them completely.

Bake until a toothpick inserted into the center of the cake comes out clean, 45 to 50 minutes. Cool in the pan on a wire rack 3 minutes, then run a knife around the edge of the cake to release it from the sides of the pan. Invert a serving plate over the cake; then turn out the cake onto the plate. Let cool 30 minutes before serving.

White Chocolate–Banana Cream–Coconut Pie

MAKES 8 SERVINGS

This dessert has everybody's favorite things all rolled into one—chocolate, bananas, whipped cream, and coconut. White chocolate and ripe bananas are a perfect match.

FOR THE PIE CRUST:

1½ cups chocolate-flavored graham cracker crumbs

1 tablespoon dark brown sugar

4 tablespoons unsalted butter, melted

Preheat the oven to 350°F. Mix all the ingredients well in a medium bowl and pat into a 9-inch pie plate. Bake 10 to 12 minutes. Let cool completely on a rack at room temperature.

FOR THE FILLING:

1 cup whole milk

⅓ cup sugar

3 large egg yolks

2 tablespoons cornstarch

1 tablespoon cold unsalted butter, cut into 2 pieces

1½ ounces white chocolate, finely chopped

1 teaspoon vanilla extract

1 large banana, sliced into ¼-inch pieces

Bring the milk and 2 tablespoons of the sugar to a boil in a medium saucepan over medium-high heat. In a medium bowl, whisk together the egg yolks, remaining sugar, and cornstarch until blended. Slowly whisk the hot milk into the egg mixture and return to the saucepan. Cook over medium heat until the mixture begins to bubble. Continue cooking for 1 minute longer. Remove from the heat and add the butter, white chocolate, and vanilla, and whisk until smooth.

Place the banana slices in a single layer over the bottom of the pie crust and pour the white chocolate custard over them. Cover the surface of the custard with plastic wrap and refrigerate until completely cooled and firm, 4 hours or overnight.

FOR THE TOPPING:

1 cup very cold heavy cream
2 tablespoons sugar
½ teaspoon vanilla extract
½ cup toasted coconut (see Note)

Place the cream, sugar, and vanilla extract in a medium bowl and beat to soft peaks with a hand-held mixer.

Just before serving, top the pie with the whipped cream and the toasted coconut.

NOTE: To toast coconut, spread evenly on a sheet pan and place in a preheated 325°F oven until golden, 7 to 10 minutes. Toss or stir the coconut halfway through.

243

Key Lime Pudding Cake

MAKES 8 SERVINGS

My version of this American classic is influenced by the tropical flavor of limes straight from the Florida Keys. It is best served warm, with a dollop of rich whipped cream.

FOR THE PUDDING CAKE:

1½ cups sugar

½ cup flour

¼ teaspoon salt

6 large eggs, separated

2 cups milk

1 tablespoon lime zest

⅓ cup fresh or bottled Key lime juice

Preheat the oven to 345°F. Butter a 3-quart shallow baking dish or a 9-inch square baking dish.

Combine the sugar, flour, and salt in a medium bowl. In another medium bowl, beat together the egg yolks, milk, lime zest, and lime juice. Pour the egg yolk mixture over the flour mixture and stir until blended.

Using a hand-held electric mixer, beat the egg whites in a medium bowl until they form soft peaks. Gently fold the whites into the lime mixture and pour into the prepared baking dish.

Place the baking dish in a slightly larger roasting pan, set on the center rack of the oven, and pour in enough hot tap water to reach about halfway up the sides of the baking dish. Bake until the surface of the pudding cake is lightly golden, 40 to 45 minutes. Cool in the pan on a wire rack for 30 minutes.

FOR THE WHIPPED CREAM:

> 1 cup very cold heavy cream
>
> 2 tablespoons sugar
>
> ½ teaspoon vanilla extract

Place the heavy cream, sugar, and vanilla extract in a medium bowl and beat to soft peaks with a hand-held mixer.

Serve the pudding cake warm with a dollop of whipped cream on top of each piece.

RUSTIC FRESH PEACH PIE WITH BROWN SUGAR–ALMOND ICE CREAM

MAKES 8 SERVINGS

You have to make a fresh peach pie at least once in the summer, with all those fragrant, juicy peaches tempting you at the height of their season. This one is wrapped in a simple, unstructured crust and served with generous scoops of the best homemade ice cream.

FOR THE BROWN SUGAR–ALMOND ICE CREAM:

> 2 cups sliced almonds
>
> 1 vanilla bean, split
>
> 1 cup milk
>
> 2 cups heavy cream
>
> ¾ cup brown sugar
>
> 8 egg yolks

(continued)

Preheat the oven to 350°F. Place the almonds in a single layer on a baking sheet and bake until golden brown, 10 to 12 minutes, stirring once for even browning.

Place the milk and cream in a medium saucepan. Add the vanilla bean and 1 cup of the almonds and bring to a simmer over medium heat. Remove from the heat and let steep, covered, for 30 minutes. Strain the mixture, discarding the almonds and reserving the vanilla bean. With a small, sharp knife, scrape the vanilla seeds into the cream mixture.

Whisk together the brown sugar and egg yolks in a medium bowl. Gradually whisk in the cream-vanilla mixture, pour into a medium saucepan, and cook, stirring, over medium heat until it coats the back of a wooden spoon. Strain through a fine strainer into a medium bowl set into a larger bowl of ice water and stir until cool. Process in an ice-cream maker according to the manufacturer's instructions. Fold the remaining cup of almonds into the ice cream, spoon into a 1-quart container, and freeze until firm, from 4 hours to 1 day. Makes 1 quart.

FOR THE PIE CRUST:

2 cups all-purpose flour
¼ teaspoon salt
¾ cup cold unsalted butter
3 tablespoons cold vegetable shortening
¼ cup cold orange juice

Combine the flour, salt, butter, and shortening in a food processor and pulse until the mixture resembles coarse meal. Add the orange juice by tablespoons and continue pulsing just until the dough comes together. Wrap the pastry and refrigerate from 1 hour to 1 day.

Lightly flour a work surface and roll out the dough into a 9-inch circle that is about ⅛ inch thick. Transfer the circle to a parchment-lined baking sheet, cover with plastic wrap, and refrigerate from 30 minutes to 1 day.

246

FOR THE FILLING:

- **4 large slightly underripe peaches, peeled, pitted, and cut into ¼-inch slices**
- **2 tablespoons peach preserves**
- **2 tablespoons fresh lemon juice**
- **2 tablespoons light brown sugar**
- **3 tablespoons cornstarch**
- **½ teaspoon cinnamon**
- **2 tablespoons heavy cream**
- **1 tablespoon sugar**

Preheat the oven to 350°F. In a large bowl, mix together the peaches, preserves, lemon juice, brown sugar, cornstarch, and cinnamon until combined. Spoon the mixture into the center of the chilled pastry circle, leaving a 2-inch border all around, and fold the pastry three-fourths of the way over the filling. Brush the top of the crust with the cream and sprinkle with the sugar. Bake until golden brown, 35 to 40 minutes.

Slice and serve warm, topped with a scoop of ice cream. The ice cream will melt just a bit over the warm pie.

BAKED ALASKA—BANANA SPLIT PIE

MAKES 8 SERVINGS

My earliest job in the food world was at the counter of Baskin-Robbins. Some people might have become anti-ice cream because of all that exposure, but not me—I couldn't wait to finish work and devour their eight-scoop sundae, the Matterhorn. This chocolate-banana-strawberry-caramel ice-cream pie transports me back to those days.

FOR THE CRUST:

2 cups chocolate-flavored graham cracker crumbs

6 tablespoons unsalted butter, melted

2 tablespoons light brown sugar

¼ cup finely chopped toasted pecans (see Note)

Preheat the oven to 350°F.

Combine all the ingredients in a medium bowl, then pat onto the bottom and up the sides of a 9-inch deep-dish pie plate. Bake until set, 10 to 12 minutes. Cool on a rack; then place in the freezer for 30 minutes.

FOR THE FILLING:

1 banana, sliced ½ inch thick

2 pints premium strawberry ice cream

¾ cup finely chopped ripe pineapple

½ cup premium caramel sauce

Place the banana slices in an even layer over the chilled pie crust. Spread the ice cream evenly over the bananas and drizzle with the caramel sauce. Top with the pineapple and place in the freezer until completely frozen, about 2 hours.

FOR THE MERINGUE:

3 large egg whites, at room temperature
½ cup sugar
¼ teaspoon cream of tartar
Pinch of salt
½ teaspoon vanilla extract

Bring a large pot of water to a simmer over medium heat. Place the egg whites, sugar, cream of tartar, and salt in a large bowl and whisk to combine. Place the bowl over the simmering water and whisk until the sugar has melted and the mixture is hot to the touch, 3 to 4 minutes. Remove the bowl from the pot and using a hand-held mixer, beat until soft peaks form. Add the vanilla extract and continue beating until the egg whites are glossy and have formed stiff peaks.

Preheat the broiler. Place a rack in the top third of the oven.

Remove the pie from the freezer and, working quickly, spoon the meringue all over the filling, mounding it in the center and making sure to spread it all the way to the outer rim, so it touches the crust. Place the pie on the middle oven rack and bake until the meringue is golden brown, 4 to 5 minutes.

Freeze the pie for at least 1 hour.

NOTE: To toast pecans, place on a baking sheet in the preheated 350°F oven and toast until golden, 7 to 8 minutes, tossing halfway through.

Watermelon, Grilled Peach, and Blackberry Salad with Honey-Yogurt Dressing

MAKES 8 SERVINGS

Grill the peaches for this fruit salad to caramelize their natural sugars and bring out their flavors, but don't grill too long—you want them to keep their shape and texture. Everything else is uncooked, so you get the juicy pink watermelon and the deep, dark berries, along with the caramelized peaches, all pulled together by the creamy yogurt sauce.

FOR THE HONEY-YOGURT DRESSING:

1 cup vanilla yogurt, drained (see Note 1)
2 tablespoons honey
1 tablespoon fresh lemon juice

Combine all the ingredients in a small bowl. May be refrigerated up to 2 days. Makes about 1 cup.

FOR THE SALAD:

4 ripe peaches, halved and pitted
2 tablespoons vegetable oil
8 wedges of ripe watermelon
1 pint of blackberries
¼ cup mint, chiffonade (see Note 2)
½ cup slivered toasted almonds
   (see Note 3)

Preheat a gas or charcoal grill to medium high.

Brush the peaches on both sides with oil and grill cut-side down until golden brown and caramelized, 3 to 4 minutes. Turn over and grill 1 to 2 minutes more.

Arrange all the fruit on a large platter, drizzle with the Honey-Yogurt Dressing, and sprinkle with the mint and the toasted almonds.

NOTES:

1. To drain yogurt, place it in a cheesecloth-lined strainer over a bowl for 1 hour, until thickened. Discard the liquid that remains in the bowl.

2. To cut mint into chiffonade (fine ribbons) roll up leaves and cut into thin strips.

3. To toast slivered almonds, place on a baking sheet in a preheated 350°F oven until golden, 7 to 8 minutes, turning so they don't burn.

Vanilla Ice Cream Swirled with Fresh Berry Puree

MAKES 8 SERVINGS

What could be better than cold, rich vanilla ice cream, slightly softened and combined with sweet, fresh berries?

1 pint blackberries (substitute other berries, if you like)
½ cup sugar
2 tablespoons fresh lemon juice
1 quart premium vanilla ice cream, slightly softened

Combine the blackberries, sugar, and lemon juice in a medium nonreactive bowl. Let the berries macerate, covered, at room temperature until the juices have run, about 1 hour. Gently mash the berries with a spoon.

Place the softened ice cream in a large bowl and fold in the berry mixture.

251

8. DRINKS

For a great party, put a drink in people's hands—whether or not it's alcoholic—as soon as they arrive. Take advantage of ripe seasonal fruits that are bursting with sweetness, such as peaches and berries, as well as sweet and tart orange, lemon, lime, and pineapple juices, to mix up some gorgeous potions. Use only the best-quality ingredients in your drinks the way you use them in your food. If you're making a margarita, squeezing fresh limes into it makes all the difference in the world.

In pairing beverages with grilled foods and their accompaniments, focus on crispness—with something sizzling, you want a crisp drink. If you're serving white wine, make it a sauvignon blanc. If you're mixing up a sangria, base it on a sauvignon blanc or Spanish alvarino.

My liquors of choice are tequila or rum that have been touched with fruit juices. Although they aren't included in any of the recipes that follow, vodka and gin are good summer spirits, too. Serve them very cold with a lot of crushed ice or ice cubes. And of course, cold beer is the historic accompaniment to sizzling food, hot off the fire.

Make sure you have a good blender and a generous supply of ice ready for drinks like the Mesa and Cactus Pear Margaritas, the Frozen Peach Bellini, or the thick and frosty Banana Colada. These are irresistible mixtures with lots of flavor and punch, but most important, they are thirst quenching. And buy extra of everything you're going to need. You don't want to run out, and you want everybody to be happy while they are grilling and eating.

JERRY'S TEQUILA PUNCH

MAKES 8 SERVINGS

I created this refreshing, citrusy drink to serve with brunch. It's dedicated to Jerry Kretchmer, my partner at Mesa Grill and Bolo and the person who first saw my potential, back when I was working at Miracle Grill. Since he does so many important things for the restaurants behind the scenes, I thought Jerry deserved to have his name on the menu.

2 cups white tequila

2 cups cranberry juice

2 cups grapefruit juice

2 cups orange juice

8 orange slices

Combine all the ingredients in a pitcher and garnish with the orange slices. Serve over ice.

Passion Fruit Sangria

MAKES ABOUT 12 CUPS

I was preparing to make a White Peach Sangria on Martha Stewart's TV show when I realized I had no white peaches. Martha suggested using passion fruit instead, and it was a great idea, giving the drink a flavor that is a little sweet, a little tangy.

2 bottles dry white wine (sauvignon blanc or Spanish alvarino)

¾ cup brandy

½ cup triple sec or other orange liqueur

¾ cup simple syrup (see Note 1)

¾ cup passion fruit puree (see Note 2)

1 cup fresh orange juice

3 oranges, sliced into thin rounds

2 lemons, sliced into thin rounds

3 green apples, cored and thinly sliced

1 cup blackberries, sliced into halves

Combine all the ingredients in a large pitcher and refrigerate, covered, 2 hours to 2 days. Serve over ice.

NOTES:

1. To make simple syrup, cook equal parts of sugar and water over low heat until clear. Boil for 1 minute.

2. Passion fruit puree and juice are available at Asian and Hispanic markets and some supermarkets.

255

Mesa Margarita

MAKES 4 SERVINGS

Here is the famous margarita that *New York* magazine named New York's best. I can't think of a better welcome for your guests.

These quantities fit easily into a blender; rather than doubling them to serve eight, just make the recipe twice.

8 ounces white tequila

4 ounces triple sec or other orange liqueur

4 ounces freshly squeezed lime juice

1 cup ice cubes

1 lime wedge (optional)

Coarse salt (optional)

Process the tequila, triple sec, lime juice, and ice in a blender until smooth.

Rub the rims of 4 glasses with the lime wedge and dip into a saucer of coarse salt, if using. Divide the tequila mixture among 4 glasses.

Cactus Pear Margarita

MAKES 4 SERVINGS

Cactus pears have a tart-sweet flavor and a beautiful magenta color that adds a lot of character to a classic margarita. I first saw them used in drinks in Phoenix, Arizona, at the Phoenician Hotel.

8 ounces white tequila

4 ounces Cointreau or another orange liqueur

4 ounces cactus pear juice

2 ounces Rose's lime juice

1 cup ice cubes

1 lime wedge (optional)

Coarse salt (optional)

Process the tequila, Cointreau, pear and lime juices, and ice in a blender until smooth. Rub the rims of 4 glasses with the lime wedge and dip into a saucer of coarse salt, if using. Divide the tequila mixture among 4 glasses.

257

Frozen Peach Bellini

This is my summertime version of the classic Bellini that originated in Venice. It has lots of peach flavor and the sparkle of champagne. For additional servings, make more than one batch successively.

8 ounces champagne or other sparkling white wine

4 ounces peach nectar

2 scoops peach sorbet

1 cup crushed ice

Peach slices

Place the champagne, peach nectar, sorbet, and ice in a blender and blend until smooth. Pour into 2 glasses and garnish with peach slices.

BANANA COLADA

MAKES 4 SERVINGS

A smooth Banana Colada is so thick and frothy, it's almost a meal in itself. It certainly can be a dessert, so serve it either before or after your grilled meal. For additional servings, make more than one batch successively.

2 ripe bananas, peeled and quartered

18 ounces unsweetened pineapple juice

4 ounces sweetened coconut milk (Coco Lopez)

4 ounces dark rum

2 cups crushed ice

¼ cup toasted coconut (see Note)

Place the bananas and pineapple juice in a blender and blend until smooth. Add the coconut milk, rum, and ice and blend until frothy. Pour into 4 glasses and garnish with toasted coconut.

NOTE: To toast coconut, spread evenly on a sheet pan and place in a preheated 325°F oven until golden, 7 to 10 minutes. Toss or stir the coconut to turn, halfway through.

9. MENUS

The grill brings everything together. Somehow even disparate dishes seem to join forces and complement one another when they come off the fire seared dark golden brown, tempting us with their smoky, spicy aromas. That's why arranging these menus was so easy—you can make a fantastic meal out of almost any combination of foods in this book. You might want to try a few of my favorite matches, among them, a choice of burgers and two all-vegetable feasts, but even after you've exhausted the list that follows, your choices still will be unlimited.

When I serve burgers to my guests, I like to give them options—in this case, beef or tuna. I'm never surprised when people ask for both, so this menu allows for the heartiest of appetites.

Hamburgers with Double Cheddar Cheese,
Grilled Vidalia Onions, and Horseradish Mustard

Tuna Burgers with Pineapple-Mustard Glaze
and Green Chile–Pickle Relish

Spicy Cucumber Pickles

Red Chile-Dusted Potato Chips

Chocolate-Raspberry "Fudgesicles"

Grilled Yellow Tomato–Yellow Pepper Soup
    with Torn Corn Tortillas

Grilled Flatbread with Ricotta Cheese, Fresh Tomatoes,
    Basil, and Roasted Garlic Oil

Grilled Corn and Sweet Onion Salad

Watermelon, Grilled Peach, and Blackberry Salad
    with Honey-Yogurt Dressing

Charred Corn Polenta with Grilled Tomato Vinaigrette

Wild Mushrooms with Crushed Hazelnuts and Garlic

Grilled Cherry Tomato and Watercress Salad
    with Green Garlic Vinaigrette

Key Lime Pudding Cake

Barbecued Chicken Quesadillas with Grilled Tomato Salsa
    and Buttermilk Dressing

Red Snapper Grilled in Corn Husks with Roasted
    Jalapeño–Lime Butter

Grilled Eggplant and Pepper Salad with Cumin-Dusted Tortilla Chips

Mango-Coconut Macadamia Crisp

Ginger-Marinated Shrimp with Toasted Sesame
    Seed Vinaigrette

Spit-Roasted Duck Laquered with
    Spicy Orange Glaze

Napa Cabbage and Sesame Seed Slaw

Vanilla Ice Cream Swirled with Fresh Berry Puree

Lobster Tails with Curry-Mango Butter

Corn Niblets with Lime Butter and Tarragon

Mesa Grill Potato Salad

White Peach Melba Buckle

Squid with Grilled Tomato–Bread Salad

Tuna Steaks Brushed with Fresh Mint,
    with Fig and Nectarine Relish

Toasted Israeli Couscous Salad with Grilled
    Summer Vegetables

Lemon-Blueberry Upside-Down Cake

Grilled Sea Scallop Ceviche

Lobster Rolls with Curried Mayonnaise

Grilled Sweet Potato and Green Onion Salad

Rustic Fresh Peach Pie with Brown Sugar–
    Almond Ice Cream

Grilled Shrimp Cocktail with Tomato-Horseradish
    Dipping Sauce

Grilled Chicken Cobb Salad with
    Smoked Chile–Buttermilk Dressing

Grilled Yellow Tomato–Yellow Pepper Soup
    with Torn Corn Tortillas

Watermelon, Grilled Peach, and Blackberry Salad
    with Honey-Yogurt Dressing

Grilled Eggplant and Pepper Salad with Cumin-Dusted
Tortilla Chips

Porterhouse Steak with Tamarind Barbecue Sauce
and Basil-Marinated Tomatoes

Grilled Mushroom and Potato Salad with
Dijon Mustard Dressing

Frozen Mocha Cooler

Littleneck Clams Steamed in Green Chile–
Coconut Milk Broth

Hoisin-Marinated Pork Chops with Pineapple–
Green Onion Relish

Grilled Red Onion and Cucumber Salad
with Yogurt-Mint Dressing

Key Lime Pudding Cake

Red-Hot Marinated Chicken Skewers
with Yogurt-Cilantro Sauce

Moroccan Spice–Rubbed Leg of Lamb
with Apricot Chutney

Corn on the Cob with Red Chile–
Green Onion Butter

Grilled Cherry Tomato and Watercress
Salad with Green Garlic Vinaigrette

White Chocolate–Banana Cream–
Coconut Pie

INDEX

269

271